D1058524

BENNY TATE

WHEN YOU *Follow* A STAR AND *Find* A STABLE

RIVERSTONE GROUP PUBLISHING

DEDICATION

I would like to dedicate this book to my Rock Springs Church family. For all that has been accomplished, I give God the glory and you the credit. The privilege has been mine.

We came to Rock Springs in 1990, and you took us in.
You opened your hearts; you became our friend.
You shared all the joys, troubles, and sorrows.
We faced each day and planned for tomorrow.
As months grew into years, our lives merged together.
We formed a kinship that will last forever.
When we joined our hands to serve our Father above,
We created a circle...a circle of love.
When sorrows and illness came to our home,
You've been right there beside us to help us along.
Lifting us up in prayer and oh, so much more,
So many blessings have come to our door.
All these precious memories we will keep from day to day.
We thank the church for helping us face our doubts and fears.
You'll never know what peace and comfort we felt
Just knowing that you were near.
You each share a very special place in our hearts.
In a circle of love, you all had a part!

Rock Springs Church family, thank you for the happiest years of my life!

Pastor Benny

ACKNOWLEDGEMENTS

To my wife Barbara for believing in me when I didn't. The greatest decision I ever made was to marry you. I love you with all my heart.

To the joy of my life, my daughter Savannah Abigail. Someone said, "Children make a rich man poor"; but in my case, Savannah, you made a poor man rich. I am honored to be your dad.

To Julie Pharr, my administrative assistant. You and I both know you are more responsible for this book than I am. Thanks for working with me and making me look better than I am. You are the best! Thanks a million!

To the greatest staff on earth: Cameron, Ricky, Brian, Steve, Linda, Betty, Deb, Mildred, Ron, and Toni. Some staff are showhorses, but you are workhorses! Thanks from the bottom of my heart. What you do makes a difference.

To Ernest Pullen and the Riverstone Group for being people of excellence and integrity.

Lastly, I give all the honor and glory to the Lord Jesus Christ who saved a nobody from the wrong side of the tracks and has used me in ways I would never have believed. If He can use me, He can use anybody.

Copyright © 2005 by Benny Tate, Griffin, Georgia
All rights reserved.

No part of this publication may be reproduced, stored in a retrieval system,
or transmitted in any form or by any means except for brief quotations in
printed reviews without prior written permission by the author.

ISBN

Design and Production
Riverstone Group, LLC, Canton, Georgia

Manuscript edited by Carolyn Cunningham

Scripture quotations are from the King James Bible unless noted otherwise.

Printed in Canada

CONTENTS

FOREWORD

President Ronald Reagan, referring to the opposing candidate in a presidential debate, said, "Well, there he goes again." "Well, there Benny goes again," writing another book *When You Follow a Star and Find a Stable*.

Reagan was known as the "great communicator." He was soft spoken; yet he yielded a strong and distinct message, which was easy for ordinary people to understand. They knew what he was talking about when he referred to Russia as the "evil empire." Thomas Sowell described Reagan as a man everyone knew. Even the taxi cab drivers in DC knew him.

Benny Tate is also a wonderful communicator, who uses everyday experiences, many from his own life, to help average people learn about God and come to know Him. In this book, *When You Follow a Star and Find a Stable*, Benny shares stories about people, who tried hard to accomplish a goal, only to suffer defeat, and helps us all understand how to overcome the "stable" feeling.

Benny Tate is my friend. He is someone I admire, and I often use his humor in my own messages. One of my favorite Benny quotes is "You're as confused as a termite in a yo-yo." Benny helps us understand why tithing matters when he tells the story of a man who contributed generously to the church building fund. Another, less generous man observed, "Well, you can't give enough money to get you into Heaven." "No," the faithful giver responded, "but maybe it will help someone else get there."

As others have said, Benny Tate is an original. He is a communicator. He is humorous and dedicated to delivering God's teachings in a simple way for all to understand.

Purchase and read *When You Follow a Star and Find a Stable*. You will enjoy the reading, and all proceeds from the book will go to the building fund of Rock Springs Church.

Thank you, Benny, for inviting me to write this Foreword. May God continue to bless you, Rock Springs Church, and the United States of America.

Mac Collins
Member of Congress (Ret.)
Georgia's 8th District (R)

INTRODUCTION

I wrote this book for many reasons — one being Christmas is absolutely my favorite time of the year. There is nothing that brings me greater joy than to be able to celebrate the birth of the King of Kings.

For many of us, Christmas has always been our favorite holiday because of the marvelous memories that come flooding back to our minds: a star, a stable, and a Savior; the joy of giving gifts; the smell of a freshly cut Christmas tree; the aroma of baking cookies; the millions of lights; the smile of a child; flying reindeer; jolly men in red suits; and the gathering of families around the table, counting the blessings of God.

Certainly, it is a joyous time; but I also realize Christmas is a difficult time for many. Actually, more people commit suicide during this time than at any other time of the year. Maybe you are going through a difficult time financially, emotionally, maritally, occupationally, or parentally. Maybe you don't enjoy recalling your memories of Christmas. It is my sincere desire that this book will encourage your heart and give you strength for the journey.

I realize many families this year will celebrate the holiday without those who are very dear to them because of the separation of death. I want to assure you if your loved ones knew Christ they are experiencing their best Christmas ever.

My First Christmas in Heaven

I've had my first Christmas in Heaven:
A glorious, wonderful day!
I stood with the saints of the ages,
Who found Christ, the Truth and the Way.

I sang with the heavenly choir.
Just think! I, who so longed to sing!
And oh, what celestial music
We brought to our Savior and King!

We sang the glad songs of redemption —
How Jesus to Bethlehem came
And how they had called His Name Jesus
That all might be saved through His Name.

We sang once again with the angels
The song that they sang that blest morn
When shepherds first heard the glad story
That Jesus, the Savior, was born!

Oh Family, I wish you had been here.
No Christmas on earth could compare
With all the rapture and glory
We witnessed in Heaven so fair.

You know how I always loved Christmas.
It seemed such a wonderful day
With all my loved ones around me,
The children so happy and gay.

Yes, now I can see why I loved it;
But, oh, what a joy it will be
When you, my Loved Ones, are with me
To share in the glories I see.

So Dear Ones on earth, here's my greeting:
Look up 'til the day dawn appears;
And oh, what a Christmas awaits us
Beyond all our partings and tears!

Thank you for taking your valuable time to read my book. I assure you I wrote it with you in mind.

Merry Christmas,

Benny Tate

WHEN YOU
Follow
A STAR
AND
Find
A STABLE

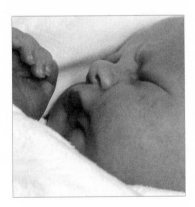

MATTHEW 2:1-12

Now when Jesus was born in Bethlehem of Judaea in the days of Herod the king, behold, there came wise men from the east to Jerusalem,

Saying, Where is he that is born King of the Jews? for we have seen his star in the east, and are come to worship him.

When Herod the king had heard these things, he was troubled, and all Jerusalem with him.

And when he had gathered all the chief priests and scribes of the people together, he demanded of them where Christ should be born.

And they said unto him, In Bethlehem of Judaea: for thus it is written by the prophet,

And thou Bethlehem, in the land of Juda, art not the least among the princes of Juda: for out of thee shall come a Governor, that shall rule my people Israel.

Then Herod, when he had privily called the wise men, inquired of them diligently what time the star appeared.

And he sent them to Bethlehem, and said, Go and search diligently for the young child; and when ye have found him, bring me word again, that I may come and worship him also.

When they had heard the king, they departed; and, lo, the star, which they saw in the east, went before them, till it came and stood over where the young child was.

When they saw the star, they rejoiced with exceeding great joy.

And when they were come into the house, they saw the young child with Mary his mother, and fell down, and worshipped him: and when they had opened their treasures, they presented unto him gifts; gold, and frankincense, and myrrh.

And being warned of God in a dream that they should not return to Herod, they departed into their own country another way.

want to share a story with you about expectations. On the first day of school, a teacher was glancing over her roll and noticed a number after each student's name such as 154, 136, or 142. *Wow! Look at these IQ's,* she thought. *What a terrific class!* The teacher promptly determined to work harder with this class than any class before. Throughout the year, she came up with innovative lessons that would challenge the students because she did not want them to get bored. Her plan worked. The class outperformed all the other classes she had taught in the usual way. During the last quarter of the year, she discovered what the numbers after the students' names really were. They were locker numbers!

Expectations are so important. Our expectations often control our conduct.

Consider the three Wise Men. When they began to follow the star, they were looking for a monarchy or a king. There is no way they were looking for a cave, which is what Jesus was born in. They were not expecting to find Him in a stable. They went to Herod's palace, looking for royalty. I wonder how they felt when they found out He was born in a stable? I have often thought that epitomizes so many people's lives. We start out following a star but sometimes find a stable.

Years ago, I preached at a youth camp in Mississippi — all week long to teenagers. I hadn't been there long when a gentleman came up to me. He looked a little older than the rest of the group; and I said, "Are you here as one of the campers?" He said, "Well, I'm actually here as the lifeguard." He was a good-looking boy — tall, dark, and handsome, seeming to have so much promise. He said, "I'm here as a lifeguard; so when the boys and girls swim, I can make sure they are safe." I said, "It's so good to meet you, Mark." I spent some time with Mark and got to know him well. He had a heart for God and was so athletic.

A few months later, I preached in Missouri; and someone said, "Brother Benny, there's a young man here who has come to see you. He said he met you in Mississippi at a youth camp." When I saw him, it was Mark. He wasn't like he was before. Mark was in a wheelchair; and he said to me, "Preacher Benny, some friends and I were out one night; and we were in a bad accident. Unless God touches me, I will be paralyzed the rest of my life and be in this wheelchair." I thought, *So much promise.* What an example of someone starting out following a star and finding a stable.

A few years ago, I preached a revival for a young pastor and his wife. They were so excited about growing their church, and I immediately became like a father to them. When we would come home from church at night, I would usually go to my room; but sometimes I would come back to the living room, and they would be wrestling in the floor! That's neat, I guess. I never did that, but I guess it's neat. I thought, *What a cute couple!*

They later called me and said, "We're going to have a baby." How exciting! Maybe wrestling leads to that. I don't know. Finally, they called me and told me the baby was born.

One Sunday night, I returned home from church and had a message from this pastor on my phone saying, "Call me as quick as you can. It's so important that you call me." I called him and asked how things were going. He said, "Things are not good. I've gone through a divorce. I've lost my wife, and I've lost my child. I didn't want it; but I think my ministry is probably over, too." I tried to encourage him; but my mind went back and I thought, *Oh, I remember when the potential looked so great.* We often start out following a star but sometimes find a stable.

Even our careers can seem promising. It appears we are excelling and doing so well, but we find a stable in our careers. Life is not a bowl of cherries; it really isn't. It's a bowl of raisins. We're raising money, raising kids, and raising cane! Sometimes you start out following a star but find a stable.

What do you do when your appointment is disappointing? We look at what the Bible says. There are three things we need to do when we start out following a star and find a stable.

First, you look for God even in the stables of life. Great people in the Bible had stables in their lives, but they looked for God even in the stables of life. Joseph was a Godly man, but his brothers sold him into slavery. He was betrayed, falsely accused, and even spent time in prison — not for being bad but for being good. Later in life, his brothers came to him and said, "Joseph, we need to apologize for what we did to you." At that time, Joseph had risen to be the second highest man in all of Egypt. Joseph said, "There's no need to apologize because what you meant for evil, God meant for good. If I hadn't gone through all that I did, we would be starving to death right now. God has orchestrated it all; and because He worked it all out, it has worked for my good." Joseph was in prison. Joseph was falsely accused. Joseph was betrayed by family, but you know what he did? He saw God even in the stables of life! We all will go through stables in life; but if we look closely enough, we will find God amidst the stables.

> I found Him blooming
> Where heartaches abundantly reign.
> Who would have dreamed
> So much joy in so much pain?
> It's good on the mountain,

> But they come and they go;
> But down in the valley,
> There's always a rose.

Job lost everything. He lost his family. He lost his livelihood. He was sick with sores all over his body. When most people would have had a pity party and given up, Job said, " . . . the LORD gave, and the LORD hath taken away; blessed be the name of the LORD" (Job 1:21).

A young man once said to me, "Brother Benny, I got the job! Praise God! He is on the throne!" I said, "Even if you hadn't gotten the job, He is still on the throne."

Paul was in a Roman prison. He had something exciting to look forward to. He was going to be beheaded in just a short time; but he wrote a letter to the church at Philippi and said in Philippians 4:4, "Rejoice in the Lord alway: and again I say, Rejoice." See, the difference between weak and strong Christians is that weak Christians only see God in the good times; but strong Christians see God in the bad times. They can see God even in the stables of life.

I went out in the hustle and bustle to do some Christmas shopping. I thought it was the time of brotherly love, but it was the time of brotherly shove! A gentleman was shopping in a wheelchair, and his legs were amputated. He sang and whistled as people rushed by. Finally, someone stopped and said, "You've lost your legs; you're in a wheelchair; and it's hard for you to maneuver out here. How do you stay happy and have such a good attitude?" The gentleman said, "I don't focus on what I've lost; I focus on what I've got left."

When we go through the stables of life, we don't need to say, "Why, God?" When we go through the stables of life, we need to say,

"Where's the star?" There is a star even in the stable. When you follow a star and find a stable, look for God in the stables of life.

Secondly, give your very best. The Wise Men thought they were going to royalty. They thought the King of the Jews might be a monarch. They could have said, "This is somewhat disappointing. Instead of giving the gold, let's give costume jewelry. Let's not give the frankincense and myrrh. We're in a stable. Let's hold back a little. We don't want to give the very best." If we're not careful, in the stables of life, we'll have a tendency not to give our very best.

"Our marriage isn't going well. He's not trying like he should. He's not doing his part. Until Meathead straightens up, I'm not going to give my best!" Does this sound familiar? "She doesn't appreciate me like she ought to appreciate me. There are lots of women who would appreciate me more than she does." Oh, if I had a nickel for every time I heard that. "She's not giving her all, so I can't give my all." When we are struggling, that is when we need to give our very best. "Down at the job, they don't appreciate me like they should. They don't give me enough money. I'm going to give them the percentage they're paying me." "No one at the church really appreciates what I do. They recognize everyone else, but I haven't gotten acknowledged one time for what I've done!"

Cathy Rigby was our hope in the 1972 Olympic Games in Munich, Germany. She was a wonderful Christian girl who loved the Lord. As she prepared for her routine, she prayed, "Lord, help me to do it with perfection. God, help me to do it with excellence." Cathy Rigby did her routine; but when they posted the scores, she didn't win. She placed her face in her hands and cried. She got in a corner and continued to cry. Her mother went over and placed her arms around

Cathy. Cathy said to her mother, "Mom, I did my best." Her mother replied, "Doing your best is more important than being the best." When you follow a star and find a stable, look for God in the stables of life but give your very best even in the stables of life.

Lastly, change your direction. Matthew 2:12 says, "And being warned of God in a dream that they should not return to Herod, they departed into their own country another way." A stable experience will change your life if you will allow it. When we go through a stable experience, the same sun that hardens the clay melts the ice. A stable experience can make you cold and callous, or it can make you caring and compassionate. We don't remember weeks; we don't remember days; we don't even remember hours. What we actually remember is moments. That is why every moment is so important. A stable experience, that very moment, can change your direction.

I've had some stable experiences in my life. When I started out, I was young and inexperienced about the ministry. When Barbara and I got married, we were young and very poor. Growing up, I was poor. I tell people I was so poor growing up that I didn't know what it was like to sleep by myself until I got married!

In my early years of ministry, I thought my job as a pastor and the secret to success was to keep everyone happy, to please everyone. I have been pastoring for more than twenty years now, and I realize I can't do that. I can't even make Barbara happy because the only person that can make her happy is herself. The only person that can make you happy is yourself. Abraham Lincoln was right: "I am as happy as I make up my mind to be." Since I thought my job was to make everyone happy, I spent six months of the year politicking and six months of the year preaching because they voted on me every year. If I made everyone mad, they would vote against me. Thank God for the day in this church when Don Thomas said, "I move we never have pastor elections again, and let Brother Benny stay as long as the Lord leads him." Thank God for that day!

There is nothing Christian about voting on individuals in church, so we don't do it. We just want to find out where you are gifted and put you in that position.

I tried everything I knew to make everyone happy, so I wouldn't offend anyone. Psalm 119:165 says, "Great peace have they which love thy law: and nothing shall offend them." If you're always being offended, you may want to check your relationship with the Lord. If you've got a chip on your shoulder, that's a good indicator there's wood higher up!

When I pastored in Tennessee, there was a lady in our community who was as lost as last year's Easter egg. She went into the hospital, and I visited her; but I didn't share Christ with her. The room was full of people, and I didn't want to offend anyone. Every time I went, the room was full. I talked about the weather or the ball game; but I never talked to her about what I should have talked to her about, and that was her soul. I was so afraid I would offend her. I didn't share Christ. I was a wimp, a politician; I just wanted to make people happy.

One Saturday afternoon as I was visiting the University of the South in Sewanee, Tennessee, God said, "Drop off the mountain, and see that lady." I said, "I'll be there Monday." If I live to be 110, I'll never forget that Sunday morning when Robert Nunley popped up on stage; walked up to me; and said, "Come here, Preacher." I walked over to Robert. He called the lady's name and said, "She died last night." I would go to bed, close my eyes, and try to sleep. I would think about this lady and wake up — perspiration all over my face and body, just sweating. I would see her burning in hell. I said, "Oh, God! I wish I had obeyed You. I wish I had been concerned, Lord, about reaching people for Jesus and been focused on what's really important."

What's really important is men, women, boys, and girls getting ready for Heaven. Truly, it's not about us; it's about them. It's about the bus ministry that tells little boys and girls about Christ because it's not about us; it's about them. I said to God, "Oh, God, if You will just forgive me, I will never do that again." That stable experience changed my direction. I look at people differently. I know the most important thing is their hearts being right with God now.

Later, I came to Rock Springs Church, my third church to pastor. People would sometimes come to me and say, "I'm depressed." I'd say, "Cheer up. Pull up your bootstraps. Dig in. Be a man. Be a woman. Cheer up." I said that until my wife went to bed for nine months with depression. When my wife went to bed and was so down, I started understanding emotional problems a little better.

A lady called me recently and said, "I just listened to you on the radio." My response is always the same: "That is so encouraging! I know there are two people listening: you and my wife." She said, "Growing up, I was sexually abused. I'm so down. I'm so depressed. You probably don't have time to listen." I said, "Yes, I have time to listen. I've got all the time you need." I'll be honest with you. I didn't have time to listen until I went through that stable experience. When you follow a star and find a stable, what God wants to do is use that stable experience to change your direction.

A dear friend of mine lost his first wife and remarried. Someone asked him what I thought was a very tacky question. They said, "Which one did you love the most: your first wife or your second wife?" I thought he gave a great answer: "Well, I really didn't know how to love until I lost my first wife." What was he saying? He was saying the stable experience changed his direction.

When we go through a stable experience, God wants us to see Him even in the stable. He wants us to give our very, very best. Then He wants to use that experience to change and conform us to be more like Jesus.

MARY
Trusted
GOD
FOR THE
Impossible

LUKE 1:26-38

And in the sixth month the angel Gabriel was sent from God unto a city of Galilee, named Nazareth,

To a virgin espoused to a man whose name was Joseph, of the house of David; and the virgin's name was Mary.

And the angel came in unto her, and said, Hail, thou that art highly favoured, the Lord is with thee: blessed art thou among women.

And when she saw him, she was troubled at his saying, and cast in her mind what manner of salutation this should be.

And the angel said unto her, Fear not, Mary: for thou hast found favour with God.

And, behold, thou shalt conceive in thy womb, and bring forth a son, and shalt call his name JESUS.

He shall be great, and shall be called the Son of the Highest: and the Lord God shall give unto him the throne of his father David:

And he shall reign over the house of Jacob for ever; and of his kingdom there shall be no end.

Then said Mary unto the angel, How shall this be, seeing I know not a man?

And the angel answered and said unto her, The Holy Ghost shall come upon thee, and the power of the Highest shall overshadow thee: therefore also that holy thing which shall be born of thee shall be called the Son of God.

And, behold, thy cousin Elisabeth, she hath also conceived a son in her old age: and this is the sixth month with her, who was called barren.

For with God nothing shall be impossible.

And Mary said, Behold the handmaid of the Lord; be it unto me according to thy word. And the angel departed from her.

*I*n studying Mary, she was a common lady with a common name. Did you know that Mary is the most common female name in America? Mary's actual name was Miriam. She was named after the sister of Moses. Mary was a common lady with a common name, but God used her in an uncommon way. God can definitely use common people in an uncommon way.

I heard an updated story about the birth of Jesus Christ. Instead of Mary and Joseph being in a stable, they were in a hospital. A school was putting on a production with Mary in the delivery room and Joseph holding Mary's hand as she had the baby Jesus. In the waiting room of the hospital were the shepherds and angelic host. A nurse took the baby Jesus and walked into the waiting room. She looked at the shepherds and the angelic host; held up the baby; and said, "It's a God!"

Well, that's just what Mary had. She had Jesus, the God of this world. God used her in an uncommonly magnificent way.

There are three aspects I want you to see about this story.

First is an amazing announcement. Visualize it in the theater of your mind. Theologians say Mary probably was a fourteen-year-old girl in a betrothal period, who was at home one night, minding her own business. Luke 1:28 says the angel Gabriel appeared to her and said, "Hail, thou that art highly favoured, the Lord is with thee: blessed art thou among women." The Bible says she was troubled; and the angel said to her, "Mary, fear not because you will bear a Son and His name will be called Jesus and He will be the Highest. He will rule over the house of David, and He will save His people from their sins."

She was a virgin girl and said, "Now wait just a minute, Gabriel. This all sounds great. I'm going to have a baby. He's going to be the Savior of the world, but there's only one problem. I've never known a man." He said, "Oh, Mary, I've got the answer for that. The Holy Ghost has overshadowed you, and the daddy to this baby is God!"

God showed me three truths about this announcement. **First, God's timing may seem wrong; but it is always right.** Timing is important. Sometimes the only thing between salad and garbage is timing! This fourteen-year-old girl probably thought, *Now here the angel Gabriel shared with me I'm going to have the Christ child; but I'm only fourteen years old, a young girl, not even officially married. This is definitely the wrong timing.*

God's timing may seem wrong, but it is always right. When God leads us to do something, it may seem like it can't be the right time; but if God is leading us to do it, it is always the right time.

God showed me this truth in my own life. I pastored the Sweeten Hill Congregational Methodist Church for three years. I left the church for health reasons — some of the deacons got sick of me! I saw the church grow from thirteen to over 200. We experienced revival; but after three years, I felt led to leave the church. The deacons said to me, "Brother Benny, we don't understand it. You could have a job here as long as you want one."

That's what's wrong with a lot of people. All they've got is a job. Instead of letting God call the shots and letting God lead and direct their lives, all they've got is a job. If all I wanted was a job, I could get one by eight tonight. You say, "I can't find work." If you believe that, don't sleep on your side tonight! You, too, can find a job by eight tonight if you're willing to work.

They said to me, "We don't understand this. Our church is doing better financially and is larger than it's ever been in our history. You've built us up; we're doing good; and now you're leaving?" I said, "I'm not deciding to leave. God is telling me to leave." God's timing is always right — even when it may seem wrong.

Secondly, God's announcement may bring fear. Luke 1:30 says, "And the angel said unto her, Fear not, Mary . . . ." Even when it's God's announcement or God's direction, there may be fear.

I love the story about the two boys who walked into a dentist's office. One boy said to the dentist, "I want to say something to you today." He looked in the dentist's eyes and said, "We don't have time to sit around here all day. We've got a lot to do. We want to go fishing; we want to play ball; and we've got a lot to do today. Doc, we've got a tooth that has to come out! Forget the Novocain; forget the gas. Just grab the pliers, and jerk that jammie out!" The dentist looked at the young man and said, "My, my, I admire your courage. Which tooth is it?" He looked over at his friend and said, "Tommy, open your mouth!" He had a lot of bravery when it came to Tommy, but I don't know how much he had when it came to himself! When God gives us an announcement — whether it's to purchase a house, have a child, sing a special, teach a Sunday School class, make an investment, or open a business — even with God's announcement, there is sometimes fear.

Thirdly, God will continue to speak to those who listen. God had spoken to Mary before. How do we know the angel Gabriel had been to Mary's house before? Luke 1:29 says, "And when she saw him, she was troubled at his saying, and cast in her mind what manner of salutation this should be." When she saw the angel Gabriel and he gave her the announcement, she was troubled — not at his appearance, not by the angelic being. She was troubled by the saying. If an angel had not appeared to her before, she would have been troubled by his appearance. She wasn't troubled by his appearance; she was troubled by what he had to say. She couldn't understand his announcement since she was a virgin. The point is God will not reveal more truth to you until you obey the truth you already know. God speaks to those who listen to Him and obey Him.

In this story, I also see an amazing assignment. When Sarah was chosen to birth Isaac, she was almost 100 years old. When Elisabeth was told she would have John the Baptist, the great forerunner of Jesus Christ, she was an elderly lady. Would you have trusted a fourteen-year-old girl, a little peasant girl, to birth the Savior of the world? It was an amazing assignment.

As I study the Scripture, it seems God always uses the unlikely people. He used fatherless Abraham to be the father of a nation. He used stuttering Moses to be the spokesman for Israel. He used undisciplined Samson to be the judge. He used unstable Peter to be the rock of the church. It seems to me God has always used the unlikely people.

It is so encouraging to me that if God can entrust a fourteen-year-old girl to birth the Messiah of the world, He can use you and me. God has a special assignment for us. In God's family, there are no big I's and no little you's; but God has a special assignment for every one of us.

I once preached at a teen camp meeting in Mississippi; and as I looked over the crowd, I saw some beautiful girls and some girls who weren't so pretty. I saw some good-looking boys and some boys who weren't so good looking. I saw some who were fit and trim and some who were like me and needed a Slim•Fast®.

I'll never forget when I connected with them. I could tell when I had touched them. A lot of churches have a clock on the back wall. I don't need a clock on the wall; I can look at the people and tell when I'm through. I could tell when I got on those young people's level. I looked them in the eye and said, "Young people, God has a special assignment for every one of you. Whether you're big, small, smart, not so smart, make good grades or bad grades, God loves you and He's got a special assignment for you."

I wish the people of God could realize they are special to Him. He's got an assignment just for you. God wants you to do something with your life. Daniel 11:32 says, ". . . the people that do know their God shall be strong, and do exploits."

If you don't know your assignment, here are three questions to ask yourself. **First, "What do I weep about? What makes me cry?"** Always remember your passion comes out of your pain. A guy says, "I've really got a passion for kids." Well, he may have a passion for kids because he had a difficult childhood. "I've got a passion to feed hungry people." Maybe it's because you went hungry when you were smaller. To determine your assignment in life, you've got to ask, "What really breaks my heart?" Often God wants you to do something to be part of the solution to the problem He shows you.

Secondly, ask yourself, "What do I sing about? What makes me happy and brings me the greatest fulfillment?" What I enjoy most is helping people. When I was able to walk in a home and look at three little children and present their father a substantial check from our church and say, "I sure hope this makes your Christmas bright," I left there on shoutin' ground! That's what it's all about — helping people.

Thirdly, "What do I dream about? What would I do with my life if I knew I couldn't fail?"

There was a special announcement; there was a special assignment; and **there was a special acceptance.** Luke 1:38 says, ". . . Behold the handmaid of the Lord; be it unto me according to thy word. And the angel departed from her." When you believe God for the impossible, you always risk some things.

When Mary believed God for the impossible, she risked four things. **She risked family rejection.** Joseph could have said, "I'm not going to marry you" and totally rejected her. Remember when David was going up against the giant? His brothers said, "Who are you? There's no way you can slay the giant. You're just a peon." If you believe God for the impossible, you're going to risk family rejection.

You'll also risk your reputation. My friend, forget about your reputation. If you're going to live for God and you're going to believe God for the impossible, you're going to risk your reputation. Mary risked her reputation. There were people whispering, and the rumors were running wild. "There's a woman who's not married, and she's going to have a child."

In addition to family rejection and reputation, **you risk your standard of living.** In Biblical times, the women were totally dependent on the men. Joseph could have said, "Mary, I'm not going to marry you."

She also risked her life. Mary could have been stoned for having a child without being married.

God chose Mary. Not only did God choose Mary, but also Mary chose God. Several years passed, and Jesus was at a wedding. Jesus' mother walked up to Him and said, "Jesus, they're out of wine." And Jesus said, paraphrasing, "That's not any of my business. My time has not yet come." Then He looked over at the servants and said, "Fill the containers to the brim." Mary said, "Whatever He tells you to do, do it. I've been through a lot with this boy. Believe me, we go back about thirty-two years! You wouldn't believe how He came into this world! You wouldn't believe the angelic being that came! After everything I've been through, whatever He tells you to do, be sure and do it!"

If Mary could speak to you and me, she would say, "Whatever He tells you to do, do it. Whatever He tells you to give, give it. Wherever He tells you to go, go there. Whoever He tells you to marry, marry them. Whatever He tells you to do, just be sure and do it." Mary believed God for the impossible.

JOSEPH
Believed
THE
BEST
IN
People

MATTHEW 1:18-25

Now the birth of Jesus Christ was on this wise: When as his mother Mary was espoused to Joseph, before they came together, she was found with child of the Holy Ghost.

Then Joseph her husband, being a just man and not willing to make her a publick example, was minded to put her away privily.

But while he thought on these things, behold, the angel of the Lord appeared unto him in a dream, saying, Joseph, thou son of David, fear not to take unto thee Mary thy wife: for that which is conceived in her is of the Holy Ghost.

And she shall bring forth a son, and thou shalt call his name JESUS: for he shall save his people from their sins.

Now all this was done, that it might be fulfilled which was spoken of the Lord by the prophet, saying,

Behold, a virgin shall be with child, and shall bring forth a son, and they shall call his name Emmanuel, which being interpreted is, God with us.

Then Joseph being raised from sleep did as the angel of the Lord had bidden him, and took unto him his wife: And knew her not till she had brought forth her firstborn son: and he called his name JESUS.

*J*oseph is probably the man in the Bible we know the least about. I am of deep conviction he is one of the most admirable men in the Bible. We know he was the foster father of Jesus Christ, but we don't know a whole lot about him.

There are two things we do know. One, he was a very poor man. In Biblical times, according to the law, on the eighth day, a child had to be circumcised. So Joseph and Mary took Jesus to the temple to have Him circumcised. The normal sacrifice for a child was a lamb, but the law allowed for very poor families to give turtledoves as a sacrifice. The Bible says when Joseph and Mary came to have Jesus Christ circumcised and to offer up a sacrifice, instead of offering a lamb, they offered two turtledoves. That tells me Joseph was a very poor man.

The second thing we know about Joseph is he was a carpenter. The Bible says in Matthew 13:55, "Is not this the carpenter's son?"

What I really admire about Joseph are the character qualities he had in his life. I think if we would focus on Joseph, we could learn so much from his character.

There are five things I admire about Joseph's character.

First is his relationship with God. Theologians say around the time Christ was born, Joseph was about thirty years of age. I have often wondered, with the millions of men throughout the ceaseless ages of time, why was Joseph chosen to be the foster father of Jesus? Why did God choose this poor carpenter? Matthew 1:19 says, "Then Joseph her husband, being a just man." In the Hebrew translation, it says, "Joseph her husband, being a righteous man." You know why Joseph was chosen to be the foster father of the Lord Jesus Christ? God was looking for someone He could trust to do what was right.

God is still looking for people to use in a great capacity who are willing to do what is right. God is looking for people who do what is right when everyone's looking or when no one's looking!

I remember going to hear Norman Schwarzkopf speak — Stormin' Norman, the leader of Desert Storm. I went to hear this great leader, and I was so excited. I pulled out my notepad and pen. I learned a long time ago if you're going to quote right, you've got to note right. I also learned a short pencil is better than a long memory. Norman said, "There are only two rules for leadership. Always remember this. The first rule is: When in charge, take control. The second rule is: Always do what's right."

God is looking for people who will do what's right. 2 Chronicles 16:9 says, "For the eyes of the LORD run to and fro throughout the whole earth, to shew himself strong in the behalf of them whose heart is perfect toward him. . . ." God chose Joseph because He could trust him to do what was right. I admire his relationship with God.

Secondly is his reaction to problems. You can tell more about a person by their reaction than you can by their action. Here, Joseph was about thirty years of age. Theologians say Mary was probably about fourteen. He saw her one day; their eyes met; and it was meant to be! Joseph said, "That's the gal for me!"

Thank God for young men and young women who are attracted to the opposite sex. Thank God! That's normal!

They started dating; and before you know it, they were in a betrothal period. In Biblical times, the betrothal period was similar to an engagement period but was much stricter. The betrothal period was a one-year period where there was no physical relationship between the man and woman. It was different from an engagement period because in Matthew 1:18, even in the betrothal, they were considered husband and wife. Also, if they separated during the betrothal period, there had to be a legal divorce. It was a serious one-year period.

During this time, Mary said, "Joseph, we need to talk." He said, "Okay." She said, "Joe, what I want to talk to you about is you and I have not had any type of physical relationship." He said, "Yes, I am very much aware of that!" He said, "We've only got two more months! Two more months!" The Bible didn't say he said that, but it didn't say he didn't!

She said, "There is something I need to talk to you about. Joseph, I'm going to have a baby." He said, "What?" She said, "Yes, I am going to have a baby; and I am going to tell you who the father is. The father is God. The father is the Holy Ghost."

Joseph could have done a lot of things. Even the law says he could have had her stoned and he could have cast the first stone. But Matthew 1:19 says he did not want to make her a public example.

What is your reaction to problems? What is your reaction when things don't go as planned?

I admire Joseph's relationship with God; I admire his reaction to problems; and **I admire his respect for Mary.** Joseph could have gone downtown and said, "Guys, let me tell you what's happened to me. Mary is going to have a baby, and I'm not the dad. Can you believe — as committed as I've been to her? Yet she would go out and do something like this?" But the Bible says the opposite. He did not want to make a public example of her. He had great respect for Mary. I have been preaching for many years now, and you can tell a lot about a man by how he treats his wife. You can tell a lot about a lady by how she treats her husband. I believe Mary said, "When I first started dating Joseph, I thought he was a great man; but now I know how great a man he really is." I admire Joseph's respect for Mary.

The fourth thing I admire about Joseph is his receptivity to God's plan. Matthew 1:20 states, "But while he thought on these things, behold, the angel of the Lord appeared unto him in a dream, saying, Joseph, thou son of David, fear not to take unto thee Mary thy wife: for that which is conceived in her is of the Holy Ghost." Verse 24 says, "Then Joseph being raised from sleep did as the angel of the Lord had bidden him, and took unto him his wife." I admire Joseph's receptivity to God's plan because sometimes it is difficult to listen to God.

Let me tell you two times when it is difficult to listen to God. **First, it is difficult to listen to God when we've already made plans.** Ever been there and done that? We go out and do something and say, "God, I need Your blessing on this." That's not how it works. Here is what Joseph probably thought, *I'll be in this one-year betrothal period. We'll have a nice wedding. All our friends will be there. They'll throw rice on us as we leave the church, and it's going to be a wonderful time. Then we'll get financially stabilized and go out and buy our first house. Then I'll have a talk with Mary, and we'll have little Joe Joe.* God's plan was different from Joseph's plan. It's hard to listen to God when we've already made plans.

Secondly, it's hard to listen to God when His plan doesn't make sense. Proverbs 3:5-6 says, "Trust in the LORD with all thine heart; and lean not unto thine own understanding. In all thy ways acknowledge him, and he shall direct thy paths." God's plan doesn't always make sense. God's plan is not always the rational or practical thing to do. God's plan is not always what seems to be in our best interest. Sometimes God will lead you to do something that doesn't make any sense because His thoughts are much higher than our thoughts and His ways are much higher than our ways.

This example is extreme, but it's a true story. There was a man in Myrtle, Mississippi by the name of Percy Ray who had a burden to start a camp. He wanted the camp to be for abused children; but more than that, he wanted it to be for abused people — people who had suffered physical, psychological, or sexual abuse. He wanted it to be a place to recover and get on with life. Percy Ray was a wonderful Christian man and had a vision of doing this but didn't have any money.

He was praying about it one night; and after he was asleep a few hours, God woke him up and said, "Percy, put on your red shirt and go out in the front yard and start digging." He nudged his wife at two in the morning and said, "Honey, where's my red tee shirt?" She said, "Who cares?" He said, "I need to put it on and go out in the front yard and start digging." She said, "Percy, it's two in the morning." He said, "Well, God is telling me to do this." She said, "Percy, what if somebody passes by and sees you?" He said, "Nevertheless, I must go."

Percy Ray went out in the front yard, started digging, and had been there about fifteen minutes when a limousine pulled up. A man got out of the limousine and said, "I've been looking for you for three days. God told me to get in my car and drive until I found a man on the side of the road in a red shirt digging. I found a lot of people on the side of the road digging, but you're the first one I've found with a red shirt on. God told me to give you a check." The man pulled out a check for a million dollars; gave it to Percy Ray; and said, "All I know is God told me to give you this toward your mission." If you go to Myrtle, Mississippi, there's a tremendous 2,000-seat facility where people come to find help for physical, emotional, and psychological recovery.

We need to obey God — even when it doesn't make sense. If you're really seeking the will of God, don't talk to twenty-five people about it. You'll be hearing so many voices you won't hear the voice of God! Get alone with God. He can give you the answer.

The fifth thing I admire about Joseph is his risk taking in the lives of others. Joseph believed in Mary when no one else believed in her. Joseph took a risk and believed in Mary. The Bible teaches us we need to be like Joseph and believe the best in people.

Do you remember in John 1:42 when Jesus came to a guy named Peter? If anyone epitomizes most of us, it's Peter. He was the unstable guy. He was always sticking his foot in his mouth. He was making sporadic decisions. He personified instability. Peter was there one day, and Jesus came to him. He called him by name and said, "Simon, the son of Jona?" He replied, "That's me, the unstable guy." Jesus looked at him and said, "No more shall you be called Simon or the son of Jona; but from now on, I want to call you Cephas." The word *Cephas* meant "a stone." When Jesus looked at Peter, he didn't see a guy who was unstable as water. He saw a leader. He saw a writer of the New Testament. He saw an apostle. He saw a man who would preach on the day of Pentecost and three thousand people be saved. He saw the best in Peter. God wants us to believe the best in people.

Motivational author and speaker Mamie McCullough writes, "I believe in you. No matter what you've done, I believe in you. No matter what's happened to you, I believe in you. No matter what people say, I believe in you. No matter if you're rich or poor, I believe in you. No matter your age, size, or IQ, I believe in you. No matter where you live, I believe in you. No matter your position or lack of one, I believe in you. No matter, no matter, no matter, I believe in you." There are scores of people out there who need someone to believe in them.

There are scores of people out there with untapped potential who could do exploits, who could speak volumes and do volumes for the kingdom of God — if they just had someone to believe in them. Joseph believed the best in people.

THE
LITTLE
Things
ABOUT
Christmas

LUKE 2:1-7

And it came to pass in those days, that there went out a decree from Caesar Augustus, that all the world should be taxed.

(And this taxing was first made when Cyrenius was governor of Syria.)

And all went to be taxed, every one into his own city.

And Joseph also went up from Galilee, out of the city of Nazareth, into Judaea, unto the city of David, which is called Bethlehem; (because he was of the house and lineage of David:)

To be taxed with Mary his espoused wife, being great with child.

And so it was, that, while they were there, the days were accomplished that she should be delivered.

And she brought forth her firstborn son, and wrapped him in swaddling clothes, and laid him in a manger; because there was no room for them in the inn.

here is no holiday that is celebrated any bigger than Christmas. It is celebrated by more people in more parts of the world than any other. I am convinced — even though it is celebrated in such big fashion — it is the little things about it that make it special.

I know it is the little things about Christmas that make it special to me. I can't wait each year to watch my favorite Christmas story, "The Homecoming." It is the story that launched "The Waltons." I love looking at the ornaments on my Christmas tree and recalling the special memories connected to each one of them. I enjoy putting banana pudding out for Santa and receiving divinity candy from a lady in our church whose grandmother made it for me years ago. I love Christmas caroling, buying gifts, and seeing the excitement in the eyes of children. When Christmas morning comes, it thrills my heart to gather with my family around the Christmas tree and read Matthew 2, sing "Happy Birthday" to Jesus, and pray and thank Him for all the gifts. Yes, it is the little things that make Christmas special.

I recently asked my wife Barbara why she married me. I said, "Was it my strong physique, vivacious personality, or my good looks?" She said, "It was your mind." "My mind?" I responded. Yes, it is the little things that count!

I want you to notice three little things in our Scripture verses. **First, let's notice the little problems.**

Joseph and Mary certainly had their share of problems, including **money problems.** Caesar Augustus had decreed that everyone should return to their homeland and register for taxation. I am sure this was a struggle for them since they were a poor couple. Remember, under the law when parents brought their children to the temple to be cir-

cumcised, they could offer a sacrifice of two turtledoves instead of a
lamb if they were very poor. That is what Mary and Joseph did. I have
often said, "Christmas is when Santa comes down the chimney and our
savings go down the drain!" Yes, in December, we have jingle bells;
and in January, we juggle bills. No doubt, Joseph and Mary had
money problems.

Secondly, they had **relational problems.** They were going to have
a baby but weren't married.

Thirdly, they had **travel problems.** Keep in mind that Mary was
close to delivering Jesus and they had to travel 100 miles from
Nazareth to Bethlehem. It is estimated the trip took around ten days
— with the travel being rough and difficult.

Fourthly, they had **lodging problems.** There was no place for
Jesus to be born. I heard about a man who went to a hotel and asked
for a room. The clerk said, "We have no vacancy." The man then
asked, "If President George W. Bush were coming tonight, would you
have a room for him?" The clerk said, "Certainly." The man said,
"Well, he's not; so I'll take that room." God told the shepherds,
through an angelic being, to go to Bethlehem and see the Savior born
in a manger. For many years, I wondered how they knew which child
was the Christ child. I am sure lots of babies were born that night in
Bethlehem. Then I realized He was the only one born in a manger.

When I read this story, it is easy to see the problems — but why
all the problems? There were 300 Old Testament prophecies concerning the birth of Jesus Christ, and every one of them had to be fulfilled
for God to fulfill His plan. That's the reason for the problems: to fulfill God's plan.

Maybe you are having some problems in your life. Did you know
it takes problems to make you more like Jesus? The Bible says in

Romans 8:28-29, "And we know that all things work together for good to them that love God, to them who are the called according to his purpose. For whom he did foreknow, he also did predestinate to be conformed to the image of his Son . . . ." Jesus was mocked, betrayed, ridiculed, denied, and forsaken. God is conforming us to His image, and that takes problems. Don't you believe the "feel good" preaching taking place today that says, "Name it, claim it, believe it, receive it, health and wealth, blab it, and grab it!" The life that pleases God is often painful and difficult. I assure you there are far more valleys than mountaintops in the Christian life. God sends us two bad days for every good day to keep us looking toward Him.

Secondly, I want us to notice the little places. I would have thought the Savior would have been born in a palace in Rome, not a barn in Bethlehem; but God uses little places. In a field, David was chosen to be King of Israel. Most of the psalms were written in caves. The Sermon on the Mount was given from a grassy hillside. Jesus spent two-thirds of His ministry on the Sea of Galilee, which was a small body of water that was six miles wide and thirteen miles long. God uses little places.

God has certainly used little places in my life. Hubbards Cove, Tennessee is not on the map; but every time I drive through it, I cry because it was there one night around midnight that I accepted Jesus. It was right there that I was born into the family of God. I have often said, "Thank God for salvation! God thought it; Jesus brought it; the Holy Spirit wrought it; the Blood bought it; the Bible taught it; the devil fought it; and in Hubbards Cove, I caught it!"

I will never forget Oak Grove Church in Tracy City, Tennessee. The church probably doesn't seat a hundred people. The building is very small; but it was in that parking lot, I asked Barbara to marry me. I wasn't from the model family. I was born out of wedlock, didn't know who my dad was, and was told by my stepfather that I was ignorant and would never amount to anything; but she believed in me when I didn't even believe in myself. I will never forget that Oak Grove Church parking lot.

I can take you to a small spot in Stone Mountain, Georgia where I held my daughter for the very first time. Barbara and I were married for nine years and could not have children. We struggled, prayed, questioned, and cried ourselves to sleep many nights; but I will never forget when I held our adopted daughter the very first time. She was three days old and in a foster home. The foster mother placed her in my arms; and as tears ran down my face, I said, "Savannah Abigail, your daddy loves you." I will never forget the foster mother looking at me and saying, "Daddy, she loves you, too." I thank God for the special little places in my life.

While I am speaking of little places, I must include my church on Rock Springs Road in Milner, Georgia. We are so far in the country that our zip code is EIEIO. We are so far out that you have to go toward town to go hunting. It's just a little spot in the road. Christian leadership consultant, speaker, and author John Maxwell once came and said, "If Jesus comes back while I am here, I hope He can find me!"

The church growth experts told us our demographics were not conducive to church growth, and it would not happen out here. However, I am thrilled to report we just completed a 1,200-seat sanctuary; have three services on Sunday; a membership of near 2,000; and have seen hundreds of people come to know Jesus Christ. I encourage pastors to not always be looking for a stepping-stone and greener grass (it may be over a septic tank), but bloom where you are planted! God uses little places.

"Father, where shall I work today?"
And my love flowed warm and free.
He pointed out a tiny spot and said,
"Tend that place for Me."

I answered Him quickly, "Oh, no! Not that!
Why, no one would ever see —
No matter how well my work was done.
Not that little place for me!"

The word He spoke, then, wasn't stern.
He answered me tenderly,
"Nazareth was a little place
and so was Galilee."

Thirdly, I want us to notice the little people. I would have thought the mother of Jesus would be the queen of Rome, not a young Jewish girl — and the father at least a scribe, not a carpenter — and the announcement of His birth to the Sanhedrin, not to a group of uneducated shepherds; but God uses little people. It seems to me God has always used the unlikely. Childless Abraham became the father of a nation; stuttering Moses became the leader of Israel; undisciplined Samson became a judge; a shepherd boy David became king; and unstable Peter became a pillar of the Church. God seems to use little people. When President Ronald Reagan received his first Bible from his mother, she wrote the following words in it: "Ronald, you can never be too small for God to use you; but you can be too big."

Hudson Taylor was asked why God used him to do such awesome

mission work in China. He responded, "God looked until He found someone small enough to do the job." The Bible is very clear that God uses those people who are little in their own sight. Samuel said to King Saul, "When thou wast little in thine own sight, wast thou not made the head of the tribes of Israel, and the LORD anointed thee king over Israel?" (1 Samuel 15:17).

A story that well illustrates this point is the experience of missionary Milton Cunningham. Milton was flying from Atlanta to Dallas. When he found his seat, it happened to be the middle seat in the section. To his right next to the window was a young girl who obviously had Down syndrome. The young girl began asking him some very simple but almost offensive questions. "Mister, did you brush your teeth this morning?" she asked. He looked rather shocked at the question but responded, "Well, yes, I brushed my teeth this morning." The girl said, "Good. That's what you're supposed to do." Then she asked, "Mister, do you smoke?" Again Milton was a little uncomfortable but told her with a little chuckle that he did not. She said, "Good 'cause that will make you die." Then she said, "Mister, do you love Jesus?" Milton was really caught off guard by the simplicity and the forthrightness of her questions. He smiled and said, "Well, yes, I do love Jesus." The young girl with Down syndrome just smiled and said, "Good 'cause we're all supposed to love Jesus."

About the time the plane was getting ready for takeoff, another gentleman sat down beside Milton on the aisle seat. He began reading a magazine. The young girl nudged Milton and said, "Mister, ask him if he brushed his teeth this morning." Milton was really uneasy with that one and said he was not going to do it. The girl continued to nudge Milton, saying, "Ask him! Ask him!" So Milton turned to the man seated next to him and said, "Sir, I don't mean to bother you; but my friend here wants me to ask you if you brushed your teeth this morning." The man looked startled, of course. But when he looked past Milton and saw the young girl sitting there, he could tell she had good intentions; so he took her question in stride and said with a smile, "Well, yes, I brushed my teeth this morning."

As the plane taxied down the runway and began to take off, the girl nudged Milton again and said, "Ask him if he smokes." And so Milton did. The man said the same thing Milton had said.

As the plane lifted into the air, the young girl nudged Milton one last time and said, "Ask him if he loves Jesus." Milton turned to the fellow once more and said, "Now she wants to know if you love Jesus?" The man could have responded like he had to the previous questions – with a smile on his face and a chuckle in his voice; and he almost did. But then the smile on his face disappeared, and his expression became serious. He turned to Milton and said, "You know, honestly, I can't say that I do. It's not that I don't want to; it's just that I don't know Him. I don't know how to know Him. I've wanted to be a person of faith all my life, but I haven't known how to do it. And now I've come to a time in my life when I really need that very much."

As the plane soared through the skies between Atlanta and Dallas, Milton Cunningham listened to the man talk about his life and was able to share his story and testimony. He told the man how to become a person of faith. It all happened because God used a young girl with Down syndrome.

Christmas is certainly a big holiday, but I believe it is the little things about it that really make it special.

✡

What MADE THE *Wise*

MEN *Wise*

MATTHEW 2:1-12

Now when Jesus was born in Bethlehem of Judaea in the days of Herod the king, behold, there came wise men from the east to Jerusalem,

Saying, Where is he that is born King of the Jews? for we have seen his star in the east, and are come to worship him.

When Herod the king had heard these things, he was troubled, and all Jerusalem with him.

And when he had gathered all the chief priests and scribes of the people together, he demanded of them where Christ should be born.

And they said unto him, In Bethlehem of Judaea: for thus it is written by the prophet,

And thou Bethlehem, in the land of Juda, art not the least among the princes of Juda: for out of thee shall come a Governor, that shall rule my people Israel.

Then Herod, when he had privily called the wise men, inquired of them diligently what time the star appeared.

And he sent them to Bethlehem, and said, Go and search diligently for the young child; and when ye have found him, bring me word again, that I may come and worship him also.

When they had heard the king, they departed; and, lo, the star, which they saw in the east, went before them, till it came and stood over where the young child was.

When they saw the star, they rejoiced with exceeding great joy.

And when they were come into the house, they saw the young child with Mary his mother, and fell down, and worshipped him: and when they had opened their treasures, they presented unto him gifts; gold, and frankincense, and myrrh.

And being warned of God in a dream that they should not return to Herod, they departed into their own country another way.

I heard a story about three men who were marooned on a deserted island. They were on the island for about twenty years and had made the best of it, but one day they were very depressed. They were despondent, dismayed, and said, "Why me?" They noticed a bottle had floated up in the lagoon. They grabbed the bottle, opened the top, and out popped a genie. The genie said to the men, "I will give each of you one wish. Instantly, as you share that wish with me, it will be granted." The first man said, "I wish I was back in Boston working in my office." He no more said it; and he was back in Boston — behind his desk, working. The other man said, "I would like to be back in Dallas, Texas — gathered around the table with my family, spending quality time and sharing a meal with them." He no more said that and zoom! He was back in Dallas, Texas. Then she looked at the third man and said, "What about you?" He said, "Well, I have to be honest with you. Since one of my friends has gone to Boston and the other has gone to Dallas, I'm very lonely. I wish my friends would come back." Sure enough, before you knew it, the three men were back on the deserted island! I can tell you that third guy was not very wise. I think I used to be his pastor!

There are four things that made the Wise Men wise.

First was the Person they sought. Two thousand years later, wise men still seek Jesus. The Wise Men saw a star in the east; and they traveled 1,500 miles from Mesopotamia to Bethlehem to see the Christ child.

We don't know a lot about these Wise Men, but we do know three things about them. **First, they were wise.** They were astrologers and astronomers, and they interpreted dreams. Even today, ninety percent of astronomers believe in God. It is the highest percentage of any occupation. Why do they believe in God? Because they look into the heavens and see they declare the glory of God. They were intelligent men, but they still needed a Savior. You can be smart and well educated, and you can have more degrees than a thermometer; but you still need a Savior! The Bible says in Psalm 111:10, "The fear of the LORD is the beginning of wisdom . . . ." In 2 Timothy 3:7, the Bible says, "Ever learning, and never able to come to the knowledge of the truth." James 1:5 says, "If any of you lack wisdom, let him ask of God . . . ." They were Wise Men, but they still needed a Savior.

Not only were they Wise Men, but **they were wealthy men.** We know they were wealthy men not only because they were astrologers but also by the gifts they brought. They brought expensive gifts. They were wealthy men, but they still needed a Savior. Michael Jordan — with all of his endorsements — made over 78 million dollars a year; but he still needs a Savior.

It's amazing to me — all these athletes, who make so much money, especially football players. You look on the field, and there's twenty-two guys fighting over a ball when they all could afford to buy their own!

Matthew 6:19-20 says, "Lay not up for yourselves treasures upon earth, where moth and rust doth corrupt, and where thieves break through and steal: But lay up for yourselves treasures in heaven, where neither moth nor rust doth corrupt, and where thieves do not break through nor steal." Matthew 16:26 says, "For what is a man profited, if he shall gain the whole world, and lose his own soul? or what shall a man give in exchange for his soul?"

Someone asked me, "Where are we in Bible prophecy, Pastor?" I'll tell you where we are. In Revelation 4:1, the rapture takes place. I'm a very impatient person, and I've often thought I'm going to love the rapture because zoom — we're gone! The rapture takes place in Revelation 4:1; and we are in Revelation 3:17 right now, which says, "Because thou sayest, I am rich, and increased with goods, and have need of nothing; and knowest not that thou art wretched, and miserable, and poor, and blind, and naked."

It was a great day in my life when I realized the most important things in life are not things and that happiness is not *having* the best of everything but happiness is *making* the best of everything! The only difference between men and boys is the price of their toys. A lot of people think if they can get that new car or that new home, they'll be happy; but let me tell you something: Wherever you go, there you are. It's not wrong to possess things; but for many people, they aren't possessing things — things possess them. They buy things they don't need with money they don't have to impress people they don't like.

They were Wise Men; they were wealthy men; and **they were well-born men.** They were descendants of Daniel. If you study the Bible, there are two men who you can't find a flaw in their character: Joseph and Daniel. They were well-born men. They could have said, "We don't need Jesus. Our forefather was Daniel." Your forefathers and your grandparents may have been wonderful people. Your parents may be wonderful people, but you still need a Savior. See, here is what you have to realize: God has no grandchildren; He only has children. What made the Wise Men wise was the Person they sought.

The second thing was the perils they fought. They had to go through a difficult journey. They didn't see the star one day in Mesopotamia and the next day end up in Bethlehem. They traveled 1,500 miles. They crossed the Euphrates River. They crossed a hot desert because they wanted to see Jesus. Life can't be all sunshine, or the flowers would die. If we're going to make it to Jesus, sometimes it's a difficult journey. Jerry Falwell says the life that pleases God is often painful and difficult. God never promised everything would go well. He never promised us a smooth flight, but He did promise us a safe landing.

Not only did they experience a difficult journey, but also **they encountered deadly jealousy.** In Matthew 2:7-8, Herod said to the Wise Men, "What time did the star appear?" He said, "When you go to Bethlehem, be sure and send me back word. I want to come and worship Jesus also."

Herod was a different type of guy. He was married ten times. Now that tells you he had psychological problems.

A lady walked up to a man and said, "My, my, I don't mean to stare at you so much; but you look just like my third husband." He said, "Ma'am, how many times have you been married?" She said, "Twice!"

Herod would have the Jewish people butchered; and while they were literally being killed, he would lick his lips and clap his hands and say, "Death be to them." He was so insecure he had three of his biological sons killed because he thought they desired his throne. He contracted a sexually transmitted disease and got very sick. He knew he was dying; so three days before he died, he said to his men, "Capture all of the Jews that you can, and treat them royally. Treat them wonderfully; but the instant I die, kill every one of them." So when these Wise Men came and said, "We are hunting the King of the Jews," they were literally risking their lives. They went through a difficult journey, and they went through deadly jealousy. No matter what we go through, it's worth it to get to Jesus.

✡

The third thing that made the Wise Men wise was the plan they were taught. They were taught the reading of the Scriptures. They traveled 1,500 miles and came from Mesopotamia to Jerusalem. Once they got to Jerusalem, they said, "Where is He?" Herod called the scribes together; and the scribes said, "Well, if you had just read Micah 5:2, you would have known where He is. Micah 5:2 says He will be born in Bethlehem." When the Wise Men needed direction, all they needed to do was get into the Bible.

You say, "Well, I am facing a major decision; and I need some direction for my life." Psalm 119:105 says, "Thy word is a lamp unto my feet, and a light unto my path." To find Jesus, all you need to do is get into the Bible. Nineteenth-century American evangelist D. L. Moody, founder of the Moody Bible Institute in Chicago, said, "God didn't give us the Bible to increase our knowledge, but He gave us the Bible to change our lives." If you need direction in your life, certainly get into the Word.

They were taught the reading of the Scriptures, and they were taught to rely on the Savior. These men had followed the star for 1,500 miles; they were intelligent men; and they knew that stars moved east to west. When they got to Jerusalem, they said, "Where is He?" They said this because that is as far west as the star went. They were leaning to their own understanding and knowledge. God circumvented nature, and the star not only went east to west; but the star went north to south five miles from Jerusalem to Bethlehem.

What is the message for you and me? Sometimes God leads us to do things that don't seem natural and don't seem normal that everybody else might not understand. I wish people would quit thinking they need society's opinion before they obey the Lord! What we need to do is keep our eyes on the star! If God says go, we need to go. If God says no, we need to no.

They learned the reading of the Scriptures; they learned to rely on the Savior; and they learned the restraining of the Spirit. We see this in Matthew 2:12: "And being warned of God in a dream that they should not return to Herod, they departed into their own country another way."

Often people don't realize that God restrained them through the Holy Spirit. People will come to me and say, "Pastor, God has opened a wonderful door!" I will say, "Praise God! That's great! I'm excited for you!" God does open doors, but sometimes God closes doors. We should be just as excited when He closes the door as we are when He opens the door. People say, "God has brought a wonderful friend into my life. We have such a wonderful relationship." God will bring people into your life, and God will move people out of your life. I have been guilty of this for so long, but God moves people out of my life. They want to get off the train; and I go back to them and say, "Get back on the train. Come on. Go with me. I'm taking a journey." It's a great day in our lives when we realize God moves people into our lives but also moves them out. If God closes the door, don't crawl through the window!

The fourth thing that made the Wise Men wise was the presents they brought. If there was ever a time when Mary was worthy of some admiration, instead when the Wise Men came to the house, they worshipped Jesus. Not Mary, not Joseph Smith, not Confucius, not Buddha; but they worshipped Jesus. I will tell you who was worthy of worship; and that is Jesus, the Lamb of God. He is the only One worthy of worship and worthy of praise.

If there is anything we need to give Jesus, we need to give Him praise. The only thing you can give Him is praise. You say, "I'm going to give Him my life"; but He gave you life. You say, "I'm going to give Him my tithe"; but He gave you the money. The only thing you can give Him that He didn't give you is praise.

A mother read this story to her little boy from Matthew 2, and she was asking Johnny questions about the story. She said, "Johnny, what did the Wise Men bring to Jesus? What were the three gifts?" He said, "Well, Mom, it was gold, Frankensteins, and Smurfs!" Well, that's close.

The Wise Men did bring gold. Why did they bring gold and give it to Him? Gold was a gift appropriate only for a king. Revelation 19:16 says, "And he hath on his vesture and on his thigh a name written, KING OF KINGS, AND LORD OF LORDS." When they brought that gift and laid it at the feet of baby Jesus, Jesus — being probably two years old — they were saying to Him, "You are King of Kings, and You are our Lord of Lords."

Not only did they bring gold, but they also brought frankincense. Why did they bring frankincense? Frankincense was used by the high priest in worship when he was offering up atonement for the sins of the people. When they brought frankincense and laid it at the feet of Jesus, they were saying to Jesus, "You *are* our High Priest." Hebrews 4:14-15 says, "Seeing then that we have a great high priest, that is passed into the heavens, Jesus the Son of God, let us hold fast our profession. For we have not an high priest which cannot be touched with the feeling of our infirmities; but was in all points tempted like as we are, yet without sin." When they offered the frankincense, they were saying, "Jesus, everything we will ever encounter in life, You will encounter. You will set the precedents; and You will show us how to handle betrayal, heartache, and discouragement because You are our High Priest."

The last gift they brought and laid at the feet of Jesus was the gift of myrrh. The reason they brought the gift of myrrh was because myrrh was used in embalming bodies. When they placed the gift of myrrh at the feet of Jesus, they were saying, "Jesus, this myrrh represents death. Jesus, thank You for coming. Thank You for growing up. Thank You for living thirty-three and a half years. After that, Jesus, we know You will die on an old rugged cross a vicarious death for all the people of the world."

Christmastime is my favorite time of the year. We're decorating our trees and putting our gifts under our trees. God put up His tree, and He didn't place His gift under the tree; He placed His gift *on* the tree. Jesus bled and died that every one of us might have a right to eternal life. I just can't get over that. I love preaching about the birth of Jesus Christ, but I've read the Bible through and through. Not one time are we told to remember the Babe of Bethlehem; but over and over and over, we are told to remember the Christ of Calvary. I don't want to get over what Jesus Christ did for me. The Wise Men brought their gifts and gave them to Jesus.

I wonder today what do we need to give Jesus? Some of us need to give Him our hearts, surrendered lives, our families, our baptisms, our church memberships, our tithes, our time, or our talents. My friend, we need to give our gifts to Jesus. **He is worthy!**

✡

THE
Grinch
WHO
Tried to
STEAL
Christmas

MATTHEW 2:1-18

Now when Jesus was born in Bethlehem of Judaea in the days of Herod the king, behold, there came wise men from the east to Jerusalem,

Saying, Where is he that is born King of the Jews? for we have seen his star in the east, and are come to worship him.

When Herod the king had heard these things, he was troubled, and all Jerusalem with him.

And when he had gathered all the chief priests and scribes of the people together, he demanded of them where Christ should be born.

And they said unto him, In Bethlehem of Judaea: for thus it is written by the prophet,

And thou Bethlehem, in the land of Juda, art not the least among the princes of Juda: for out of thee shall come a Governor, that shall rule my people Israel.

Then Herod, when he had privily called the wise men, inquired of them diligently what time the star appeared.

And he sent them to Bethlehem, and said, Go and search diligently for the young child; and when ye have found him, bring me word again, that I may come and worship him also.

When they had heard the king, they departed; and, lo, the star, which they saw in the east, went before them, till it came and stood over where the young child was.

When they saw the star, they rejoiced with exceeding great joy.

And when they were come into the house, they saw the young child with Mary his mother, and fell down, and worshipped him: and when they had opened their treasures, they presented unto him gifts; gold, and frankincense, and myrrh.

And being warned of God in a dream that they should not return to Herod, they departed into their own country another way.

And when they were departed, behold, the angel of the Lord appeareth to Joseph in a dream, saying, Arise, and take the young child and his mother, and flee into Egypt, and be thou there until I bring thee word: for Herod will seek the young child to destroy him.

When he arose, he took the young child and his mother by night, and departed into Egypt:

And was there until the death of Herod: that it might be fulfilled which was spoken of the Lord by the prophet, saying, Out of Egypt have I called my son.

Then Herod, when he saw that he was mocked of the wise men, was exceeding wroth, and sent forth, and slew all the children that were in Bethlehem, and in all the coasts thereof, from two years old and under, according to the time which he had diligently inquired of the wise men.

Then was fulfilled that which was spoken by Jeremy the prophet, saying,

In Rama was there a voice heard, lamentation, and weeping, and great mourning, Rachel weeping for her children, and would not be comforted, because they are not.

*D*r. Seuss's *The Grinch Who Stole Christmas* is probably one of the best-known Christmas stories. Whether you've seen the original cartoon or the movie, most of us are familiar with the story. As I researched the movie, I found more than 100 million dollars were spent on makeup alone.

We know there is no such thing as a group of people called the Who's with disfigured noses and twelve toes. There is no such thing as a town called Whoville, and we all know there is no such thing as a Grinch. However, there *are* people who behave like a Grinch. There are people who talk like a Grinch and who hurt like a Grinch. The Grinch was pretty easy to identify. He had a green, hairy body; and he looked different from everyone else; but the Grinches we come into contact with may not be so easy to identify. I am convinced they look normal and dress normal. I am convinced that many times they have a wife, two kids, and a dog. They talk like us, act like us, look like us; but yet they're Grinches. There might just be a Grinch in your midst today.

How do you identify a Grinch? There are some indicators in Matthew 2.

First of all, you know you are a Grinch if you get upset when others invade your territory. In the beginning of *The Grinch Who Stole Christmas*, the people are singing Christmas songs, blowing their whistles, and beating their drums. Everyone is happy about Christmas — except the Grinch. He is standing up on the mountain, looking down over Whoville, saying, "I had a bad experience down in Whoville, and I came up here to make my home in this cave because I wanted to get away from all that. I wanted to get away from the singing and the whistles and the drums. I wanted to get away from Christmas, but they have invaded my territory!"

There was a man in Matthew 2 whose territory was invaded. His name was Herod. The Roman Senate gave him the title "King of the Jews." He took great pride in being King of the Jews. He was a powerful and prestigious man. He was also a very paranoid man. He was so paranoid that he had three of his sons killed because he thought they wanted to take over his throne. He had his wife killed because he thought she was orchestrating a plan to overtake him. When the Wise Men traveled 1,500 miles and said to Herod, "We have seen His star in the east and have come to worship the *King of the Jews*," that statement troubled him. Not only did that statement trouble him, but a better word is that statement torqued him. Why was he torqued? Someone had invaded his territory.

Many times, that is how we are. We're okay until someone invades our territory. We're okay, but we're not going to deal with our anger problem. We're okay, but we're not going to deal with our impure thinking. We're okay, but we're not going to talk about the feelings we have towards that person. We're okay, but we're not going to lay our finances on the table. Many times we're okay until someone invades our territory.

We've often heard, "The truth never hurt anybody"; but that's not true. The truth does hurt.

A preacher said, "We need to quit smoking cigarettes!" One sister said, "Amen, Preacher. Preach on!" Then he said, "We need to quit smoking cigars!" She said, "Good preachin'! Come on, Brother!" Then he said, "We need to do away with our snuff!" She said, "He's quit preachin' and gone to meddlin' now!"

How is it for us when we come to church and God invades our territory? You might be a Grinch if you get upset when someone invades your comfort zone or your territory.

Another indicator you might be a Grinch is if you pretend to be something you're not. The Grinch said, "I'm hated down there in Whoville. Those Whovillians, they don't like me." But that wasn't true. There was a girl named Cindy Loo who thought he was great. The devil will tell you that nobody likes you. The Grinch thought for a minute and said, "There's somebody down there they do like. Ho! Ho! Ho! They like Santa Claus." So he got a red suit and a hat and dressed up like Santa Claus; but he wasn't Santa Claus. He was just pretend.

Herod said, "Where is this King of the Jews supposed to be born?" The scribes said, "If you study the law, He is supposed to be born in Bethlehem." Herod said to the Wise Men, "You go to Bethlehem; and when you locate Him, be sure and let me know because I want to come there and worship Him." Herod did not want to worship Him. According to verse 13, he wanted to kill Him. See, you might be a Grinch if you pretend to be something you're not.

We do a lot of pretending during Christmas with people we haven't seen in eleven months and twenty-nine days. We say, "I can pretend to like them for just one night." We hug and embrace and say, "It's so good to see you!" If it's so good to see them, why don't we see them more? Just a thought. We go to office parties with coworkers we despise, but we pretend for just one night. Then we walk into church like we're Ward and June Cleaver. We pretend we've got the most wonderful home. Reality is we are so far from that. Our relationship is strained; our home life isn't good; but we've got to keep up the façade. We've got to keep pretending. If nothing else, we do it for the kids' sake. We just keep pretending. The pastor walks up to us after we argued all the way to church and says, "How are you doing?" We say, "Great!" You might be a Grinch if you pretend to be something you're not.

A third sign you might be a Grinch is if you can't join others in their joy. Remember, the Grinch put on the Santa Claus suit and had an idea. He said, "I'll go to Whoville and take away all their presents." He couldn't find a reindeer but saw his old dog Max. He put some horns on Max and went south to load up all the presents. The Whovillians were happy, but he couldn't join them in their joy.

Matthew 2:10 says, "When they saw the star, they rejoiced with exceeding great joy." Herod knew Christ was to be born in Bethlehem. The Wise Men went to Bethlehem because they wanted to experience the joy and exuberance of seeing the precious Son of God. You know what is so interesting to me? It's only five miles from Jerusalem to Bethlehem, but Herod didn't go with them. He could have traveled five miles. He could have been there, but he couldn't join them in their joy. You might be a Grinch if you have a problem joining other people in their joy.

Let me give you the status of the church. We weep pretty well together. "I'm sorry your wife left you. I'm here for you." "I'm sorry you've been diagnosed with cancer. I'm here for you." We weep pretty well together, but we don't rejoice well together. Someone said, "It's difficult to save money when your neighbor keeps buying things you can't afford." "Did you hear about so and so? They got a beautiful new house." *"I don't want the payment."* "Did you hear about that family? They got a new BMW." *"I hear it's a used one."* "I'm so excited! She got the role in the play." *"Yeah, but the teacher has her picks."* "Have you heard about so and so? She looks so good. She's lost a lot of weight." *"Yeah, but I hear she's taking diet pills."*

Maybe that's why the Grinch was green because he was eaten up with envy. In Romans 1:28-32, the Bible talks about some gross sins. It talks about murder, fornication, haters of God; and then it includes a little four-letter word *envy*. We might be a Grinch if we can't join others in their joy.

A fourth indicator you might be a Grinch is if you get infuriated when things don't go your way. God warned the Wise Men not to go back to Herod. Then God warned Joseph to take Mary and the Christ child to Egypt. Do you know when this happened? Matthew 2:16 says Herod was so torqued he had called for every baby in Bethlehem under two years of age to be killed. The Bible says Herod was very upset. He was infuriated when things didn't go as he planned!

The Grinch went down to Whoville the night before Christmas and put all the presents on his sled. He hooked up ole Max and beat him till he got to the top of the cliff. He said, "For Christmas morning, we'll drop the sled with all the toys and presents on it; and they'll be destroyed!" You know the story. It didn't go like the Grinch had planned.

How are you when things don't go like you planned? How are you when you don't get your way? How are you when everyone doesn't conform to your schedule?

Lastly, you might be a Grinch if your heart has never been changed. The Grinch said, "I can't wait for Christmas morning! They won't have their presents and they won't have their gifts and they're going to be so upset!" Christmas morning came down in Whoville. Some of the people were upset; but there was a girl named Cindy Loo who said, "I'm glad it happened. I'm glad the Grinch has taken all of our gifts because it's important we realize Christmas isn't about gifts. It's about what's in our hearts." I wish, as Americans, we could realize Christmas isn't about gifts. It's about the greatest gift, the precious Son of God, the unspeakable gift God has given for every one of us. The people said, "Cindy Loo, you're right"; and they started singing songs. About that time, the ole Grinch heard them and said, "I thought they would be upset. I thought they would have given up with no gifts, but they're still celebrating Christmas." You remember what happened next. The Grinch's heart was two sizes too small. After the Grinch's heart grew three sizes, he began to cry. He said, "Max, I feel all toasty inside." Then he took his hands; reached up to his eyes; and said, "I'm leaking." He looked over at Max and said, "Max, I love you."

This is where the parallel stops. Throughout this story, we have paralleled the Grinch and Herod; but Herod never had a heart change. According to verses 19 and 20, Jesus' family did not come back to Jerusalem until after Herod died. Right up until Herod's death, he had a desire to kill the Christ.

What do people need? They need a heart change. Romans 10:9-10 say, "That if thou shalt confess with thy mouth the Lord Jesus, and shalt believe in thine heart that God hath raised him from the dead, thou shalt be saved. For with the heart man believeth unto righteousness; and with the mouth confession is made unto salvation." If you want to go to Heaven, what do you need to do? Give your heart to Jesus Christ.

✡

GIFT
Worth
GIVING

MATTHEW 2:1-18

Now when Jesus was born in Bethlehem of Judaea in the days of Herod the king, behold, there came wise men from the east to Jerusalem,

Saying, Where is he that is born King of the Jews? for we have seen his star in the east, and are come to worship him.

When Herod the king had heard these things, he was troubled, and all Jerusalem with him.

And when he had gathered all the chief priests and scribes of the people together, he demanded of them where Christ should be born.

And they said unto him, In Bethlehem of Judaea: for thus it is written by the prophet,

And thou Bethlehem, in the land of Juda, art not the least among the princes of Juda: for out of thee shall come a Governor, that shall rule my people Israel.

Then Herod, when he had privily called the wise men, inquired of them diligently what time the star appeared.

And he sent them to Bethlehem, and said, Go and search diligently for the young child; and when ye have found him, bring me word again, that I may come and worship him also.

When they had heard the king, they departed; and, lo, the star, which they saw in the east, went before them, till it came and stood over where the young child was.

When they saw the star, they rejoiced with exceeding great joy.

And when they were come into the house, they saw the young child with Mary his mother, and fell down, and worshipped him: and when they had opened their treasures, they presented unto him gifts; gold, and frankincense, and myrrh.

And being warned of God in a dream that they should not return to Herod, they departed into their own country another way.

And when they were departed, behold, the angel of the Lord appeareth to Joseph in a dream, saying, Arise, and take the young child and his mother, and flee into Egypt, and be thou there until I bring thee word: for Herod will seek the young child to destroy him.

When he arose, he took the young child and his mother by night, and departed into Egypt:

And was there until the death of Herod: that it might be fulfilled which was spoken of the Lord by the prophet, saying, Out of Egypt have I called my son.

Then Herod, when he saw that he was mocked of the wise men, was exceeding wroth, and sent forth, and slew all the children that were in Bethlehem, and in all the coasts thereof, from two years old and under, according to the time which he had diligently inquired of the wise men.

Then was fulfilled that which was spoken by Jeremy the prophet, saying,

In Rama was there a voice heard, lamentation, and weeping, and great mourning, Rachel weeping for her children, and would not be comforted, because they are not.

he tradition of gift giving started more than 2,000 years ago with the Wise Men who came from the east and brought gifts of gold, frankincense, and myrrh. I want to tell you about a gift worth giving.

There are three types of gifts we give at Christmastime.

First of all, we give a gift-for-a-gift gift. What is a gift-for-a-gift gift? It's when you know someone is going to buy you a gift and you try to anticipate: *I wonder how much they're going to spend on me?* And you think: *I sure hope I can get them a gift comparable to what they've spent on me because I sure don't want to feel uncomfortable when we open gifts.* We've all given a gift-for-a-gift gift. You've done it. You go to the mailbox; get a Christmas card out; and say, "Oh my goodness, I wouldn't have thought they would send me a card!" So you run in and get a card and mail it to them. You've been there; done that; and got the belt buckle and tee shirt to prove it, right? We've all given a gift-for-a-gift gift. What's bad is when you get the card on December 24th and it's too late to mail one back before Christmas!

We also give a gift-for-a-favor gift. It's when the person isn't expecting a gift in return, but they are expecting a favor. You know, down at the company, when you walk out and they hand you a ham or a turkey. They aren't expecting you to get them a ham or a turkey. It would be kind of wild if everybody did one year though, wouldn't it? What they're expecting is a favor. They expect you to work hard. They expect you to speak well of the company. They expect a good job performance. It's a gift-for-a-favor gift.

Lastly is a grace gift. In Ephesians 2:8-9, the Bible says, "For by grace are ye saved through faith; and that not of yourselves: it is the gift of God: Not of works, lest any man should boast." A grace gift is what God bestowed on us when He sent His Son Jesus Christ. It is an unrepayable gift; it is a grace gift.

Grace gifts are usually nonmaterial. When I was a boy, I used to give grace gifts to my mother. Christmas would come, and it seemed like December was no different than the other eleven months. I never had any money. So when I knew my mother would be gone for several hours, I would clean the house. I even polished the furniture! I had that house looking as immaculate as I possibly could. My mother would return; and I would say, "Mama, it's Christmastime. I didn't have any money to buy you a gift, but I've cleaned the house. I think everything looks real nice." She would say to me, "Well, Benny, that means more to me than anything you could have bought." What was it? It was a grace gift.

Back home in Tennessee, there was a couple in my church by the name of Harvey and Elizabeth Howell. They were such precious people. He was eighty, and she was in her late seventies. I would go up to Mrs. Howell's, and she would fix me great meals that I loved so much. When I was getting ready to leave Tennessee, she gave me a big hug and said, "I'm sure going to miss you." I said, "We're sure going to miss you too, Mrs. Howell." She said, "I'll tell you what I'm going to do. I know you're going to get homesick once you're in Georgia; so for the first year and a half you're there, I'll write you and Barbara a letter every week. I'll tell you everything that is going on in our community. I'll keep you abreast of everything. You can look for a letter from me once a week." She was exactly right. For a year and a half, once a week, she sent us a letter. I looked so forward to getting that letter from Mrs. Elizabeth Howell in the mailbox every week! That was a grace gift! It was a nonmaterial gift, and there was no way I could ever repay her for that grace gift.

It is also impossible to measure the cost of a grace gift. After I pastored at Rock Springs Church for a couple of months, I was really homesick. You've never been sick until you've been homesick.

I remember one Sunday I was standing at the back of the sanctuary as people were leaving the service. Mr. Alvis and Mrs. Norma Butler came out the door. I said to her, "God bless you, Mrs. Norma." She said, "God bless you, Pastor. You're homesick, aren't you?" I said, "Yes, I really am." She said, "You're considering loading up everything you've got and going back to Tennessee, aren't you?" I said, "To be honest, it's crossed my mind." She said, "We don't want you to go back to Tennessee. We want you to stay right here. I want you to come up to our house, and I'll be your mama." I did go up to her house, and she was my mama. She was a mother to Barbara and I both. Not only was she a mother to us, but she was a grandmother to Savannah. I would walk in her house, and she always kept M&Ms and nuts just inside the door. She would tell Barbara, "You need to buy nuts. Benny likes nuts." I would walk in and get me some nuts, and I would deliberately look at the refrigerator because she had all of her grandchildren on it. Right in the middle of the pictures of her grandchildren would be a picture of Savannah. For Savannah's birthday, Mama Butler would come bringing a gift. I'd say, "Mama Butler, you don't need to do that." She'd say, "Well, I do it for all of my grandchildren." I wouldn't do it in front of her, but that just made me have a running spell! She saw a young couple with a baby, away from their family, who needed support; and she gave them a grace gift. I could never repay her for that. When you think about doing something good for someone, you need to get shopping off your mind and give them a grace gift!

I was in a meeting in Atlanta, Georgia with Barbara and the biological mother and father of Savannah, along with her biological grandparents. Bethany Christian Services, the largest Christian adoption agency in the world, said, "We've never heard of a meeting like this." We met for two hours. It was obvious I was the talker in the family, so they directed all the questions to me. For hours, they asked me questions about everything imaginable. They asked me where I stood concerning the Smurfs and where I stood concerning mythology. For two hours, they popped questions at me. I finally got tired of the questions, looked at the family, and said, "You picked us out of a profile book. You saw our pictures and our bios. There were lots of other families to choose from, but you picked us. There were lots of families who monetarily could give your baby more than we could, but I want you to know something. Nobody in the profile book can give your baby any more love than we can." They said, "We want you to be the adoptive parents of our baby." That was a grace gift. I could never thank that little blond-haired girl and that little red-haired boy enough for the gift they bestowed upon Barbara and I. It was a grace gift. We all need to learn to give some grace gifts.

There are six truths we learn from the Wise Men about giving.

First, give an unexpected gift. Here are Joseph and Mary, who obviously are poor because when they offered up a sacrifice for Jesus at eight days old, they couldn't offer up a lamb. They had to offer up two turtledoves. Little did they know there would be a caravan of astrologers bringing gold, frankincense, and myrrh to their humble home eighteen months later. They did not expect the gift they were given.

You know what I believe God wants us to do this year? I believe

God wants us to give an unexpected gift. Why don't we search for someone who's really not expecting us to do something for them? Why don't we search for someone who we know is not going to do anything for us and give them a gift?

Secondly, give a gift with genuine joy. Matthew 2:10 says, "When they saw the star, they rejoiced with exceeding great joy." One man said, "God, You can have anything You can pry out of my hand." God, help us not to give grudgingly. Help us to give a gift with genuine joy and understand it is more blessed to give than to receive. Don't be an old grouch! Give with joy!

Third, give a personal gift. The gold they gave was a gift appropriate for a king. Jesus was the King of Kings and Lord of Lords. Frankincense was what the high priests used in worship; so they were saying, "You are our High Priest." Myrrh was used to embalm bodies; so they were saying, "You will die for the sins of the world." What did they do? They gave a personal gift. There were probably 300 of them. They could have just brought a ham. Better than that, they were wealthy men. Why didn't they just send their gift? Why didn't they say, "Christmas is such a busy time. I've got so much going on. I'm not going to travel 1,500 miles to cross the Euphrates River and bother with that hot desert. I'm just going to send some of our men to bring the gifts." They gave a personal gift. The greatest gifts you'll ever receive are personal gifts.

I remember in 1994 we had Pastor Appreciation Day at Rock Springs Church. I enjoyed the day and got a lot of gifts, but one gift really stuck with me. I get it out periodically to read. It's a poem by

Mrs. Mae English and it reads:

We want to show our appreciation for a pastor as nice as you,

Who shows us how much you love us by the many caring things you do.

When we asked God to send us someone, who a pastor true would be,

We didn't know He would send him from the hills of Tennessee.

The last lines say:

We love the corny jokes you tell and the laughter that they bring.

We even love to hear you when that crazy song you sing.

You are a very special person, and we thank God every day

For His providential wisdom when He sent you our way.

I don't know of any other gift I received in 1994, but I sure remember this one because it was a personal gift.

Fourth, give a gift that lasts. You know why they brought gold? In Matthew 2:13, Joseph was instructed to go to Egypt where he stayed for two years. Joseph was a very poor man and needed a way to provide for his family. What provided for him? The gold that the Wise Men brought. Where God guides, He provides; and where He leads, He succeeds. More than it lasting two years, it's lasted 2,000 years because we're still reading and singing about it 2,000 years later. We need to give a gift that lasts!

I recently read a book titled *The Power of an Encouraging Word* by Ken Sutterfield. There was a story in it about a schoolteacher in Morris, Minnesota, whose students were disruptive and saying remarks against one another. She said, "I want everyone in the class to do something. Write the name of every other student in the class on a piece of paper and skip a line." They did as she requested. She said, "Now I want you to think of the nicest thing you can about that person, and write it underneath their name." They did. She took up the papers and gave each student an individual paper with the nice things their fellow students said about them. They looked at the sheets and said, "Wow, I didn't know they thought that about me. I didn't know I meant that to them." Martin Luther said, "If you want to change your world, pick up your pen."

Years passed; and this teacher in Morris, Minnesota got a phone call from the parents of Mark Eklund. They said, "Mark was killed in Vietnam. Would you come to his funeral?" She said, "Yes, I want to do that." She went to the funeral; and after it was over, Mark's parents said, "Can we talk with you? You really made an impact on Mark when he was in the ninth grade. When Mark passed away, he had his wallet in his back pocket. We now have his wallet, and there was a piece of paper in it. The paper was tattered, torn, and taped; but it had the nice things his fellow students said about him when he was in your ninth grade class." About that time, Charlie walked up. Charlie said, "I've still got mine. I keep it in the top drawer of my desk." Then Vickie walked up and said, "I carry mine in my purse everywhere I go." About that time, another student walked up. She said, "I have mine, too. It's in my diary." We need to give a gift that lasts.

The fifth truth we learn from the Wise Men is giving will change you. Matthew 2:12 says, ". . . they departed into their own country another way." I often say, "When you give people flowers, it leaves a fragrance in your hands." Always remember that giving will change you.

✡

Lastly, we learn to give it now. One of these days is none of these days. The call we've been meaning to make, the card we've been meaning to write, the gift we've been meaning to give, the cookies we've been meaning to bake, the meal we've been meaning to prepare, the family member we've been planning to go see, do it now.

The
GIFT
Jesus
WANTS
for
HIS
Birthday

MATTHEW 2:1-12

Now when Jesus was born in Bethlehem of Judaea in the days of Herod the king, behold, there came wise men from the east to Jerusalem,

Saying, Where is he that is born King of the Jews? for we have seen his star in the east, and are come to worship him.

When Herod the king had heard these things, he was troubled, and all Jerusalem with him.

And when he had gathered all the chief priests and scribes of the people together, he demanded of them where Christ should be born.

And they said unto him, In Bethlehem of Judaea: for thus it is written by the prophet,

And thou Bethlehem, in the land of Juda, art not the least among the princes of Juda: for out of thee shall come a Governor, that shall rule my people Israel.

Then Herod, when he had privily called the wise men, inquired of them diligently what time the star appeared.

And he sent them to Bethlehem, and said, Go and search diligently for the young child; and when ye have found him, bring me word again, that I may come and worship him also.

When they had heard the king, they departed; and, lo, the star, which they saw in the east, went before them, till it came and stood over where the young child was.

When they saw the star, they rejoiced with exceeding great joy.

And when they were come into the house, they saw the young child with Mary his mother, and fell down, and worshipped him: and when they had opened their treasures, they presented unto him gifts; gold, and frankincense, and myrrh.

And being warned of God in a dream that they should not return to Herod, they departed into their own country another way.

A man and his aunt were celebrating Christmas as he excitedly opened his gift. When he did, he found a necktie — with very large checks on it. By the countenance on his face, his aunt could tell he really did not like the tie. She said to him, "I can tell you don't like the tie; but if you remember a couple of weeks ago, I asked you if you liked large or small checks." He said, "I didn't know you were talking about neckties!"

An elderly man was having a conversation with a little girl shortly after Christmas and said, "Did you get everything you wanted?" The little girl responded, "No, but that's okay. It wasn't my birthday anyway." We get so caught up in giving gifts to each other that we forget whose birthday it really is.

This tradition of giving started 2,000 years ago when astronomers from Mesopotamia brought gifts to our Lord of gold, frankincense, and myrrh. I have often thought about these Wise Men and wondered what it would have been like if they were Wise Women instead of Wise Men? First of all, they would have asked for directions. Secondly, they would have arrived on time, helped deliver the baby, cleaned the stable, made a casserole, and brought practical gifts.

Have you ever thought about what they would have said as they left? I think they would have said, "Did you see the sandals Mary was wearing with that robe?" "I can't believe they left all those disgusting animals in there!" "That donkey they were riding has seen its better days!" Here's what I'm really afraid they would have said, "That baby doesn't look anything like Joseph!"

There are some things about the Christmas story we think are true but are not. One fallacy is that the Eastern Star always represents Jesus Christ. If you think about it, they saw a star in the east and went west.

If they had gone east, they would have ended up in China or India.

A second fallacy is there were three Wise Men. The Bible doesn't say there were three Wise Men; it says they brought three gifts of gold, frankincense, and myrrh. Three Wise Men would not have troubled Herod. There were probably more like 300 Wise Men.

A third fallacy is the Wise Men came to the manger. Get real, folks. They weren't that good. They were 1,500 miles away. They traveled probably a year and a half and came to the house, not the manger. Matthew 2:11 says, "And when they were come into the house . . . ." Remember, Herod had all of the babies killed — two years old and under. Christ was apparently approaching two years of age when the Wise Men came to the house. The three gifts of gold, frankincense, and myrrh were what Jesus wanted for His birthday. Those three gifts today are still what He wants from us for His birthday.

The first gift they brought was gold. Job 23:10 says, "But he knoweth the way that I take: when he hath tried me, I shall come forth as gold." 1 Peter 1:7 says, "That the trial of your faith, being much more precious than of gold . . . ." Gold was a gift appropriate for a king. Gold symbolized commitment. What the Wise Men were saying when they brought the gift of gold was: "We are bringing acts of commitment."

"I love you, I love you, I love you," said a boy to his girlfriend. "I would scale the highest mountain or swim the widest river just to sit at your feet." But when he left, he said, "I'll come back tomorrow to see you — if it doesn't rain!"

What the Lord wants from you is commitment. He wants you to ". . . present your bodies a living sacrifice, holy, acceptable unto God

. . ." (Romans 12:1). I read the following and kept it in my Bible for a long time. It's called "Where Do You Fit In?" A national survey of churches revealed the following about church members:

10% cannot be found anywhere.

20% never attend a service.

25% admit they never pray.

35% admit they never read God's Word.

40% admit they never contribute to the church.

60% never read or study Bible lessons.

75% never assume any responsibility in the church.

95% never win a soul to Christ, but you know what is so ironic?

100% expect to go to Heaven.

What He wants from us is our commitment to Him.

A man in a World War II battle was wounded and taken to the doctor. The army doctor said to him, "I'm going to have to amputate your leg." The soldier said, "Let me clarify something right now. You're not taking off my leg. I'm gladly giving it." Now that's patriotism! That's commitment to a nation; that's commitment to a country. How much more do we need to be committed to our Lord? When we bring Him gifts of gold, we bring Him our commitment.

The second gift they brought was frankincense. Frankincense was tree gum from an Arabian tree. When it was burned, it produced a sweet odor. In Exodus 30, the Jewish people used it for worship. Frankincense represents our worship. I think we're as confused as a termite in a yo-yo when it comes to worship. I think most people come to the house of God every Sunday and never *worship*. The word *worship* comes from the old English word worth-ship. Before we can really worship God, we have to understand His worthiness.

How should worship be? Let's see how perfect worship is taking place in Heaven. Revelation 3:22 shows the end of the Church Age. In Revelation 4:1-2, the rapture of the Church takes place where Christ comes back to get His Church: "After this I looked, and, behold, a door was opened in heaven: and the first voice which I heard was as it were of a trumpet (Remember, the trump shall sound; and the dead in Christ shall rise) talking with me; which said, Come up hither, (that's the rapture of the Church) and I will shew thee things which must be hereafter. And immediately I was in the spirit: and, behold, a throne was set in heaven, and one sat on the throne." We are seeing the throne of God. Verse 3 says, "And he that sat was to look upon like a jasper and a sardine stone: and there was a rainbow round about the throne, in sight like unto an emerald." John was using his 90 A.D. terminology to describe the throne of God; but look what verse 4 says, "And round about the throne were four and twenty seats: and upon the seats I saw four and twenty elders sitting, clothed in white raiment; and they had on their heads crowns of gold." Who are these twenty-four people? Remember Jacob had twelve sons, which were the twelve tribes of Israel. Thay represent the Old Testament saints. In the New Testament, there were twelve apostles, which represent the New Testament saints. The twenty-four is symbolic of all the Old and New Testament saints. The twenty-four people represent all of us. You are a part of this group if you know Jesus Christ.

How is worship going to be? Someone said, "I need to see the future." Well, you don't need a psychic to see the future; you need to get in the Word of God! That junk is of the devil. I heard the Psychic

Network went bankrupt. You'd think they could've seen it coming! How is worship going to be? If it's going on in Heaven, that's an indicator we should be doing it down here. Look at Revelation 4:10, "The four and twenty elders fall down before him that sat on the throne, and worship him that liveth for ever and ever, and cast their crowns before the throne . . . ." You know what that tells me? When people get to Heaven, a lot of them will lose their dignity! That tells me when I get to Heaven I won't be abnormal; I'll be normal!

Revelation 4:11 says, "Thou art worthy, O Lord, to receive glory and honour and power: for thou hast created all things, and for thy pleasure they are and were created." When we come to God's house, we have to acknowledge this foundation: "God, You are worthy to get my mind totally upon You. Lord, You are worthy to sing about on the tips of my toes. God, You are worthy to get my undivided praise and receive my offering. You are worthy." What does He want from us? He wants our gold, our commitment; and He wants our frankincense, our worship.

God also wants our myrrh. Myrrh is tree gum. It produces a perfume smell and was used to prepare bodies for death. Myrrh represents death. When the Wise Men brought the myrrh, Jesus, being omniscient, knew in a short time: "I'm going to Calvary's Cross, and I'm going to die." When they placed the myrrh before Him, they said to Him, "You weren't born to live. You were born to die."

Aren't we supposed to be talking about gifts we give Him? We're supposed to give Him gold and frankincense, but His gift to us was to die for us. That gift of death He wants from us as well. Galatians 2:20 says, "I am crucified with Christ: nevertheless I live; yet not I, but Christ liveth in me: and the life which I now live in the flesh I live by

the faith of the Son of God, who loved me, and gave himself for me."
God wants us to die.

When we receive Jesus Christ as our personal Savior, it's a great
experience and we do get saved; but there's more to it than just getting
saved. We can be saved; but we still need to die out to anger, lust,
greed, bitterness, resentment, and negativity. We can be saved, but we
still need to be crucified. That is why the apostle Paul said, "I am crucified with Christ."

We need to be crucified with Christ, but we can't crucify ourselves.
Repentance is to salvation what consecration is to sanctification. All we
can do is come to Jesus and say, "To the best of my ability, I surrender
myself to You." Romans 8:13 says, "For if ye live after the flesh, ye
shall die: but if ye through the Spirit do mortify the deeds of the body,
ye shall live."

You say, "Well, how do I overcome what is eating me?" You can't
overcome it. The way you overcome it is to say, "God, to the best of
my ability, I give You all of me. Fill me with Your Spirit and Your
power because I realize it is the only way I can overcome the strong-
hold in my life." John Knox said to God, "God, give me Scotland or
I die"; and God said to John Knox, "Die and I will give you Scotland."
Whether we realize it or not, God wants us to die out to self-ambition,
self-glory, self-interest, and anger. He wants us to be crucified with
Christ. Jesus Christ died that every one of us may live! Now He is asking every one of us to die that He may live through us.

I remember the first Christmas with my daughter Savannah
Abigail. She was about four months old. We got up on Christmas
morning and did what we do every Christmas morning. I read
Matthew 2; we sang "Happy Birthday" to Jesus; and I thanked God for
all the gifts. I remember, on that first Christmas, I took a bow and

placed it on her head and said, "Girl, you are my best gift this Christmas." God wants to place a bow on our heads, and the best gift we can give Him is ourselves. What gift do you give Jesus this year?

The earth is His, the sky is too.

What can you give to Him that's new?

He is so rich because He is King.

What do you give Someone who has everything?

I'll give God me this Christmas.

It's the best thing I can give.

I'll give God me this Christmas,

And for Him I will live.

I'll give God me this Christmas

From my head down to my toes.

I'll give God me this Christmas

Because that is what He wants most.

Shepherds
WHO
Seized
THE
Moment

LUKE 2:8-20

And there were in the same country shepherds abiding in the field, keeping watch over their flock by night.

And, lo, the angel of the Lord came upon them, and the glory of the Lord shone round about them: and they were sore afraid.

And the angel said unto them, Fear not: for, behold, I bring you good tidings of great joy, which shall be to all people.

For unto you is born this day in the city of David a Saviour, which is Christ the Lord.

And this shall be a sign unto you; Ye shall find the babe wrapped in swaddling clothes, lying in a manger.

And suddenly there was with the angel a multitude of the heavenly host praising God, and saying,

Glory to God in the highest, and on earth peace, good will toward men.

And it came to pass, as the angels were gone away from them into heaven, the shepherds said one to another, Let us now go even unto Bethlehem, and see this thing which is come to pass, which the Lord hath made known unto us.

And they came with haste, and found Mary, and Joseph, and the babe lying in a manger.

And when they had seen it, they made known abroad the saying which was told them concerning this child.

And all they that heard it wondered at those things which were told them by the shepherds.

But Mary kept all these things, and pondered them in her heart.

And the shepherds returned, glorifying and praising God for all the things that they had heard and seen, as it was told unto them.

hy did God announce the birth of His only begotten
Son to shepherds? Why didn't He announce it to the
Sanhedrin, dignitaries in Israel, or the mayor and his council? I never
would have dreamed He would make this announcement to farmers.
I think there are two reasons He did.

First, shepherds were looked down upon. Shepherds were poor
and uneducated. The only occupation in Israel whose testimony was
not admissible in a court of law was that of shepherds because they had
a problem telling the truth. Luke 2:18 says, "And all they that heard
it wondered at those things which were told them by the shepherds."
This was God's way of saying, "My Son is coming and dying for everyone — rich or poor, black or white, from the right side of the tracks or
the left side of the tracks, life of obscurity, life of fame, regardless. My
Son is coming to die for everyone!" Hebrews 7:25 says, "Wherefore he
is able also to save them to the uttermost that come unto God by him,
seeing he ever liveth to make intercession for them."

**Secondly, the shepherds cared for the sheep that would be sac-
rificed for the sins of the people.** It was their job to grow sheep without spot or blemish for these sacrifices. John 1:29 says, ". . . 'Behold
the Lamb of God, which taketh away the sin of the world.' " 1 Peter
1:18-19 says, "Forasmuch as ye know that ye were not redeemed with
corruptible things, as silver and gold, from your vain conversation
received by tradition from your fathers; But with the precious blood of
Christ, as of a lamb without blemish and without spot." He was saying to the shepherds, "Guys, before you know it, you're going to be out
of work because God is sending the Lamb of Glory to die for the sins
of the world."

There are seven truths we can learn from the shepherds. **First, we need to find out what God is doing right where we are.** Let me give you some background on this situation. The taxation for the world was being set. Everyone was returning to their homeland to register, so the government could get their taxes. Joseph and Mary were returning to Bethlehem for this reason. It was a busy, hectic time — kind of like Christmastime! Amidst all the hustle and bustle, about four miles from Bethlehem, on a quiet, grassy hillside, an angel appeared and the glory of God shone round about. The greatest announcement ever to be made was given at that time!

Often we are chasing a rainbow, or we have the destination disease. We think there's going to be a certain time and place when all of the circumstances are right for God to work in our lives. I want you to know God is working in your life right now right where you are! We need to find out what God is doing right where we are because God wants to work in our lives.

Secondly, opportunities come to the faithful. Luke 2:8 says the shepherds were "abiding in the field." When I was in Israel, I watched the shepherds and their job was redundant. It seemed boring and monotonous — just a common job. Day in and day out, night in and night out, the shepherds went to their field and simply watched over their flocks. There was one night when the shepherds were watching over their flocks, and something happened. Joe looked over at Ed and said, "Ed, did you see that?" The glory of God shone round about, and an angel appeared and made the greatest announcement in the history of the world.

Opportunities come to the faithful. Where was David when he was chosen to be King of Israel? He was keeping the sheep. What was David doing when he was chosen to fight Goliath? He was bringing bread and cheese to his brothers.

If you want to be successful, note the following four steps I believe will work in anyone's life:

1. *Start to play.* Find something you enjoy doing, and do it. If you say, "I hate my job," then you need to work toward getting another one. If you hate your job, it is not God's will for you to be there. I'm not saying you quit and let your family go destitute, but you can work toward finding another job. You start to play. Proverbs 16:8 says, "Better is a little with righteousness than great revenues without right."

2. *Stop to pray.* We need to find God's will.

3. *Prepare to pay.* Everything nice has a price. Ray Kroc, the founder of McDonald's, didn't even take a salary for his first eight years of business. We need to prepare to pay.

4. *Plan to stay.* You can't quit every day or two and expect to be successful — nor can you transplant a tree every thirty minutes and expect it to produce fruit.

Thirdly, we learn new opportunities can be fearful — even though they're good. Luke 2:9-10 says, "And, lo, the angel of the Lord came upon them, and the glory of the Lord shone round about them: and they were sore afraid. And the angel said unto them, Fear not . . . ." Sometimes starting a business can be fearful — even though it is good. People say to me, "Pastor, when everything is just right, I'm going to do this; or when everything is just right, I'm going to do that." If you wait for circumstances or situations to be just right before you do something, you'll never do it. Ecclesiastes 11:4 says, "He that observeth the wind shall not sow; and he that regardeth the clouds shall not reap." There are times in our lives as Christians when we have to take risks. Courage is fear that has said its prayers.

The fourth thing we learn is God always guides clearly. Luke 2:11 tells us who was born: Jesus; for whom He was born: us; when He was born: this day; where He was born: the city of David, Bethlehem; and why He was born: because we needed a Savior.

God doesn't want His will to be a mystery to us. I don't want my will for my daughter Savannah to be a mystery. I want her to know what I expect from her and what I want for her. We are God's children. God wants us to know His will for our lives. God clearly guides. "And this shall be a sign unto you; Ye shall find the babe wrapped in swaddling clothes, lying in a manger" (Luke 2:12).

There are four principles about signs that are applicable to our lives:

1. *The greater the change, the greater the sign.* When God gave the Ten Commandments, He spoke from a burning bush that was not consumed. When Jesus was born, we had angelic announcements and stars in the sky. When Jesus died on the cross, there was a bodily resurrection. The greater the change, the greater the sign. If God has a great decision for you to make in your life, He will give you a great sign and will lead you.

2. *The greater the calling, the greater the affirmation.* If God is leading you to do something, He will affirm it through people. You may say, "I can't believe what someone said to me"; or "I can't believe who I was seated by"; or "It's so ironic I bumped into this person." God will affirm His calling to you through people.

3. *If God leads, He will precede.* If God is leading you to do something, don't be fearful. He will be there when you get there.

4. *If you obey, you will find the right way.* I have learned we must obey and go as far as we can see; and when we get there, we will be able to see farther. If God leads us to do something, we want to see it all; but it doesn't work that way. First, we obey; and then God will show us the way.

The fifth thing we learn is once you know, you need to go. Luke 2:15 says, "And it came to pass, as the angels were gone away from them into heaven, the shepherds said one to another, Let us now go even unto Bethlehem . . . ." People often want to make this spiritual and say, "I'm just waiting on the Lord"; but deep in your heart of hearts, you've known for months what you should be doing. Deep in your heart, God told you the amount of the gift you should give a long time ago. In your heart of hearts, He has dealt with you about joining the church for a long time now. "I'm just waiting on God." Even if you're on the right track, if you don't move, you'll get run over. I am saying and the Bible is saying, "Once you know, you need to go."

The sixth thing is once you go, you will know. Luke 2:16 says, "And they came with haste, and found Mary, and Joseph, and the babe lying in a manger." Once we obey God, we will look back and say, "We understand why now."

Lastly, once you find Him, you will be changed. Luke 2:20 says, "And the shepherds returned, glorifying and praising God for all the things that they had heard and seen, as it was told unto them." They went back to the same occupation; they probably looked the same; but they were changed. 2 Corinthians 5:17 says, "Therefore if any man be in Christ, he is a new creature: old things are passed away; behold, all things are become new." Once you meet Jesus Christ, you will be changed. When I met Jesus Christ, He radically changed my life. Religion can put a new suit on a man, but Christianity can put a new man in a suit! If you don't know Jesus Christ, I want you to know He can change your life. He can transform you and give you life more abundantly.

Pastor E. V. Hill told the story about a girl whose husband got converted at their church in California. A few days later on a Sunday night, she walked down the aisle. Pastor Hill asked her, "Are you coming to accept Christ?"

"No," she said, "I just want to know what's happened to my husband. He hasn't hit me in two days, and he hasn't cussed at me. What happened to him?" Someone took her aside and explained what happened to him, and she returned to receive Christ herself.

I assure you, once you meet Jesus, you will be changed.

THE
Scenery
OF
Christmas

LUKE 2:1-7

And it came to pass in those days, that there went out a decree from Caesar Augustus, that all the world should be taxed.

(And this taxing was first made when Cyrenius was governor of Syria.)

And all went to be taxed, every one into his own city.

And Joseph also went up from Galilee, out of the city of Nazareth, into Judaea, unto the city of David, which is called Bethlehem; (because he was of the house and lineage of David:)

To be taxed with Mary his espoused wife, being great with child.

And so it was, that, while they were there, the days were accomplished that she should be delivered.

And she brought forth her firstborn son, and wrapped him in swaddling clothes, and laid him in a manger; because there was no room for them in the inn.

love the scenery of Christmas. I love to go to Callaway Gardens and see eight million Christmas lights. I love the Christmas trees and the poinsettias. Legend says the poinsettia originated in Mexico, where children on Christmas Eve would bring gifts to the local church. If the local church had a Nativity Scene, they would place the gift in front of it. Supposedly, there was a girl who did not have a gift to bring; so on her way to the church, she pulled up some weeds. Legend says she placed the weeds at the foot of the Nativity Scene, and they burst into a beautiful poinsettia. Whether this is true or not, the poinsettia is still known as the flower of the Holy Night.

The following is titled "Who Says Rednecks Aren't Real Bright?"

"Hello. Is this the F.B.I.?"

"Yes, what do you want?"

"I'm calling to report my neighbor Billy Bob Smith. He's hiding marijuana in his firewood."

"Thank you very much for the call, sir."

The next day the F.B.I. agents descended on Billy Bob's house. They searched the shed, where the firewood was kept. Using axes, they busted open every piece of firewood but found no marijuana. They swore at Billy Bob and left.

The phone rang at Billy Bob's house.

"Hey, Billy Bob! Did the F.B.I. come?"

"Yeah."

"Did they chop up all your firewood?"

"Yep!"

"Merry Christmas, buddy!"

A boy told his father over and over: "I want a watch for Christmas." His father got tired of hearing it and said, "Son, I don't want to hear about that watch one more time. Better yet, if you mention that watch to me one more time, you are not going to get it!" They went to dinner; and he said, "Son, would you pray the blessing over our food?" The boy said, "Dad, I would be honored to; but would you mind if I share a Scripture before I pray the blessing?" He said, "Why no, son. Go ahead." The boy said, "Mark 13:37 'And what I say unto you I say unto all, Watch.'"

I also love Christmas scenery — my favorite being the Nativity Scene. I learned that at many of the courthouses and community centers of New Hampshire, they do not have Nativity Scenes because of the retaliation and opposition of the ACLU. I also read about something that happened in Tippecanoe County, Indiana in 1999. In front of the local courthouse, they had a Nativity Scene. The ACLU pitched a fit, and it had to be removed. A guy named Jack Ruthel didn't agree with the decision and neither do I. He put a Nativity Scene in the back of his pickup truck; and every morning at four, he went to the courthouse, pulled up in front of it, and left his truck there all day long!

One of my prize possessions is a Nativity Scene made of olive wood that I purchased in Israel. I often look at it and think about Christmas. One of these days, I will pass it down to Savannah because it is a cherished possession of mine.

There are some wonderful lessons we can learn from the Nativity Scene.

First, the Star shows us His unending light. Years ago, God guided the Wise Men to Jesus Christ; and He still wants to guide our lives. He doesn't want our lives to be a mystical maybe or a holy hunch. He has a plan for our lives! The Bible says in Psalm 119:105, "Thy word is a lamp unto my feet, and a light unto my path." God wants to be a Lamp and a Light for us to guide our lives.

A man was walking down the street and heard something say, "Stop!" He immediately stopped, and a brick fell in front of him. He kept walking and heard a voice say, "Stop!" He stopped, and a car came speeding by. Finally, he said, "Who are you?" The voice said to him, "I am your Guardian Angel. I suppose you have a lot of questions for me." He said, "Oh yes, I do! Where were you the day I got married?"

I have two observations about the star. **First, God brings stars into our lives to lead us to Jesus.** The Wise Men saw the star a year and a half before they saw Jesus and traveled 1,500 miles to see Him. God brought the star into their lives for them to see Jesus — just as God brings stars into our lives to lead us to Jesus. It may be a mom or a dad. It may be a coworker or a friend. It may be a sickness, a death, or a tragedy; but God brings stars into our lives to lead us to Jesus. 2 Peter 3:9 says, ". . . not willing that any should perish, but that all should come to repentance."

I thank God for the stars in my life like Clayton Jones, Jim McKennon, and Paul Bailey. God brought these people into my life because His ultimate plan was to lead me to Jesus. You should thank God today for the stars He brought into your life because His ultimate plan was to lead you to Himself.

Secondly, when you start following the star, you should never stop. The Wise Men were astronomers who followed the star from

Mesopotamia to Jerusalem. When they got to Jerusalem, they said, "Where is He?" Do you know what they should have done? They should have continued to follow the star.

Here is what often happens: "Oh, my Sunday School teacher is wonderful." Or "Oh, the pastor said . . ."; or "Oh, you ought to hear them sing." Let me encourage you to keep your eyes on the Star; keep your eyes on Jesus Christ, the Bright and Morning Star; because if you keep your eyes on man, he will encourage you sometimes but will discourage you as well.

They got to Jerusalem and asked, "Where is He?" because they knew stars travel east to west. They followed the star as far west as they could; but God circumvented nature, and the star traveled north to south. Bethlehem was five miles south of Jerusalem. What were they doing? They were leaning to their own understanding.

Keep your eyes on the Star. Keep looking to Jesus, the Author and Finisher of our faith. It may not seem rational or make perfect sense, but you need to keep your eyes on Jesus. Once you start following the Star, don't ever stop. The Star shows us His unending light.

The stable shows us His unsheltered life. When we picture the stable, we see the quaint, Christmassy type; but it wasn't that way. It was more like a dark, damp cave full of animals. When Jesus Christ was born, the first sounds He heard were grunts of animals. The first things He smelled were animal urine and animal dung. When they wrapped Him in swaddling clothes, that was nothing more than dust rags. Why? God — being omniscient, sovereign, infinite — why was He not born in the palace at Rome? Because God wanted Jesus Christ to understand every hurt, every perplexity, every problem, and every pain that mankind would experience. Noted nineteenth-century naturalist Henry David Thoreau, living in a hut on Walden Pond, went out into the water and squatted down until the water was at his eye level because he wanted to see the world through the eyes of a frog. God sent Jesus Christ to see the world through the eyes of a human being.

Jesus knows what it means to be born out of wedlock. He knows what it means to experience poverty. In Matthew 8:20, Jesus said, "The foxes have holes, and the birds of the air have nests; but the Son of man hath not where to lay his head." Jesus knows what it means to be discriminated against, ridiculed, mocked, abandoned by family, and rejected. He even knows what it means to suffer the physical pain of dying on Calvary's Cross. No matter what we are going through, He understands and He cares! I am so grateful that Hebrews 4:15 says, "For we have not an high priest which cannot be touched with the feeling of our infirmities; but was in all points tempted like as we are, yet without sin." I am so grateful that 2 Corinthians 1:4 says, "Who comforteth us in all our tribulation . . . ." Whatever we are going through, Jesus Christ cares and understands. He didn't live a sheltered life; He knows what it means to have adversity.

Thirdly, the manger shows us His undeniable legitimacy. The manger wasn't a bassinet; it was a feeding trough for animals. If the manger hadn't been written about in Scripture, we wouldn't know what a manger was. Because it was written about in Scripture, a feeding trough for cattle became a cradle for a King. That shows me transformation. 2 Corinthians 5:17 says, "Therefore if any man be in Christ, he is a new creature: old things are passed away; behold, all things are become new." Someone said, "I need it proven to me that Jesus Christ is real." The greatest proof I can give you is that Jesus

Christ changes people's lives. Jesus takes mangers and turns them into cradles for kings. He takes lives that are in shambles and transforms them. He radically changes people!

I went home to Tennessee recently and saw my mother and grandmother. I said, "Granny, do you know who I am?" She said, "No, sir. I don't know who you are." Alzheimer's had set in. I said, "I'm your grandson." My grandmother was a very sinful lady. She made whiskey and drank a lot of it. She went through four or five marriages. I remember, after I got saved, I started asking Granny to come to church. Granny was in her late sixties and had never been to church. I asked her repeatedly, but she wouldn't come. Finally, we were having a revival; and I said, "Granny, I wish you would come. It would tickle me if you would come to this revival. We will come get you, Granny, if you would just come with us." She said, "Well, I might go one night." She went to the revival, and the service was good! God was dealing with Granny's heart — I could just tell. It came time for the invitation; and I was praying, "Oh Lord, speak to Granny's heart. Granny needs to be saved! Please speak to her heart!" We were in a little Congregational Methodist Church with theater-type seats that popped up and down. When it came time for the invitation, her grandbaby got her leg caught in the seat. I said, "I hate you, devil" because Granny lost her focus and started concentrating on her grandbaby.

That is why I tell people that the invitation is a very sacred time. Children need to be still and be quiet. It may mean eternity for someone.

So I got her leg out and said, "You sit down and be still." In a few minutes, my grandmother started coming out. This old lady in her sixties, who didn't know Psalms from Palms, knelt down at the altar; and I prayed with her.

A few days later, we had another service. My mother had never testified; but she stood up and said, "I am a certain number of years old, and my mother got saved the other night. It was the first time in my life she ever told me that she loves me." Jesus Christ changes people's lives. For the rest of my Granny's life, she honored and glorified God. She was a wonderful Christian lady.

Recently, we went to visit my wife's father and her brother Randolph, who had just accepted Christ. Barbara said to me, "Do you know why Randolph has a beard?" I said, "No, I don't." She said, "It's from the bar fights. He was cut up in the bars, out carousing." Barbara's mother would pray for Randolph to get saved. God honored her prayers, and he got saved.

Barbara's other brother Bicki was there; and I said, "How are you doing?" He said, "I'm doing good." I said, "What about Randolph? Do you talk to Randolph much?" He said, "Yes, he calls me just about every night and says, 'Bick, why don't you come over and we'll study the Scriptures.' We'll take out our Bibles and learn about God." The guy who was in the bars. The guy whose face was cut up.

Glory be to God! Jesus Christ changes people's lives! Maybe you've tried everything else. Why don't you try Jesus?

I still believe a blood-bought, heart-felt, sin-killin', life-changin', devil-chasin' experience with God will transform men, women, boys, and girls. Our family was not from the right side of the tracks; we were from the wrong side of the tracks.

I once preached at a church in Tracy City, Tennessee; and Judge Nelson Layne came to hear me speak. I will never forget, after the service, I was standing back at the door when he shook my hand. He said, "Benny, I knew the family you were from. I knew about you all operating nightclubs and selling whiskey. I knew your family. I always thought you would stand before me, but I never thought it would be in a pulpit."

Jesus Christ changes people's lives. Jesus Christ changes people's marriages. Jesus Christ changes people's children. He is a wonderful God, and He is worthy to be praised!

THE
Christmas
TREE

ACTS 5:29-31

Then Peter and the other apostles answered and said, We ought to obey God rather than men.

The God of our fathers raised up Jesus, whom ye slew and hanged on a tree.

Him hath God exalted with his right hand to be a Prince and a Saviour, for to give repentance to Israel, and forgiveness of sins.

here is much debate about whether the Christmas tree had pagan origin or Christian origin. The pagans say it began with the Druids, who dressed up oak trees with fruit — simply to honor the gods of the harvest. The Protestants say it goes back to the year 1510 when Martin Luther was in the forest and looked up through the evergreens and saw the stars. Martin Luther said, "How beautiful." He cut down a small fir tree and placed candles on it for the children to enjoy.

I'm not sure about the origin, but I'm sure I like the Christmas tree! Notice I did not say I like putting up the Christmas tree, but I enjoy sitting and looking at the Christmas tree. I believe there is a wonderful message in the Christmas tree that may cause us to see it differently than we ever have before.

My first observation about the Christmas tree is **the lights on the tree remind us of our responsibilities.** In John 9:4-5, Jesus says, "I must work the works of him that sent me, while it is day: the night cometh, when no man can work. As long as I am in the world, I am the light of the world." That speaks volumes. Jesus has ascended to Heaven and is seated at the right hand of the Father. Matthew 5:16 says, "Let your light so shine before men, that they may see your good works, and glorify your Father which is in heaven." What that tells me is we have a responsibility to be lights in a dark and dying world.

There was a little church in France with a statue of Jesus Christ in front of the church, and Jesus was holding out His hands. During World War II, the church was bombed and the statue was destroyed. After the war, the people in this small church started rebuilding the statue. They built it back just as it had been, but there was a problem. They

could not find the hands. Everything on the statue was intact, but the
hands were not there. Finally, they put a plaque by the statue that read:

> Christ has no hands but our hands
> To do His work today.
> He has no feet but our feet
> To lead men in the way.
> He has no tongue but our tongue
> To tell them how He died.
> He has no help but our help
> To bring men to His side.

When we look at the Christmas tree and we see the lights, it
should remind us we have a great responsibility. I am convinced our
responsibility is fourfold.

Number one, our responsibility is influence. I read a statistic
years ago that said, "Just a common, ordinary person will influence
10,000 people in the course of a lifetime." I like what Abraham
Lincoln said, "God must have loved common people because He made
so many of them." It matters not if you're a housewife or the president
of a company, we all influence someone. God is saying He wants us to
use that influence for Him and for good. Whatever arena you're in,
whatever occupation you have, God says we have a responsibility to use
our influence for God and for good.

Another part of our responsibility is intercession. 1 Samuel
12:23 says, ". . . God forbid that I should sin against the LORD in ceas-
ing to pray for you . . . ." 2 Chronicles 7:14 says, "If my people, which
are called by my name, shall humble themselves, and pray, and seek my
face, and turn from their wicked ways; then will I hear from heaven,
and will forgive their sin, and will heal their land." Matthew 26:41
says, "Watch and pray, that ye enter not into temptation: the spirit

indeed is willing, but the flesh is weak." We have a responsibility of prayer and intercession. We have a responsibility to pray for our families. David said in Psalm 72:15 concerning his son, "I will praise him daily and pray for him continually." Not only do we have a responsibility to pray for our families, but we also have a responsibility to pray for people who don't know Jesus Christ. Romans 10:1 says, "Brethren, my heart's desire and prayer to God for Israel is, that they might be saved." We have a responsibility to pray for our family members and friends who don't know Jesus Christ. According to 1 Timothy 2:1-2, we've even got a tremendous responsibility to pray for those who are in authority — our leaders. When we see the lights on the Christmas tree, they should remind us of our responsibilities.

We also have the responsibility of involvement. 1 Peter 4:10 says, "As every man hath received the gift, even so minister the same one to another, as good stewards of the manifold grace of God." The Christian life is not a spectator sport. We all have the responsibility of involvement. I'm flesh and blood; you're flesh and blood; and we're all to be involved in the Lord's work. It's not like the pastor will stand before God and you won't. Your responsibility is just as great as mine. We all have a responsibility to roll up our sleeves and get to work!

I love Christmas music, and one of my favorite Christmas recordings is "Light Your World" by New Song:

> Two doors down,
> One rocking chair is rocking.
> She sits there all alone,
> Her husband dead and gone.
> The best years of her life
> They spent together.
> He was always strong,
> But now she is on her own.

And the telephone never rings.
No one laughs; no one sings.
It's quiet there.
Does anyone care?
A knocking at her door
Breaks the silence.
She looks out to see
A little boy from down the street.
She cracks the door,
Surprised that he came over.
Flowers in his hand,
Like a little gentleman.
He said, "I picked these just for you.
I hope you like the color blue.
Could I stay awhile?
I love to see you smile."
It only takes a little time
To show someone how much you care.
It only takes a little time
To answer someone's biggest prayer.
Light your world.
Let the love of God shine through
In the little things you do.
Light your world.
And though your light may be
Reaching only two or three,
Light your world.

We all have the responsibility of involvement. I travel all over preaching to churches, and it doesn't matter who the pastor is. He can preach like Billy Graham or Charles Stanley; but if the people don't realize they have the responsibility of involvement and get up off their blessed assurance, the church will not do anything.

Our fourth responsibility is investment. We have a responsibility to give of our resources. Most people want to make all they can, can all they can, and then sit on the can! That's not what the Scripture teaches. Malachi 3:10 says, "Bring ye all the tithes into the storehouse, that there may be meat in mine house, and prove me now herewith, saith the LORD of hosts, if I will not open you the windows of heaven, and pour you out a blessing, that there shall not be room enough to receive it."

To give to our new building would really be a bad investment. The bank told me, "We hope we don't ever have to repossess your building." I said, "I do, too." They said, "What would we do with a 1,200-seat auditorium?"

When we receive a manger offering and bring our gifts to the manger, I don't see a building. I see little boys and girls who need Jesus. I see teenagers who are at an age to make a decision and go either way. I see families who need to be put back together. I see senior citizens who need to be ministered to. I'm not giving to a building; I'm giving to people. I'm investing in people. My financial investments haven't done so well over the last few years. The only thing I've invested in that's doing well is the Lord's work. Yes, the lights of the Christmas tree remind us of our responsibilities.

Observation number two is the star and the ornaments on the tree remind us of our relationships. Grandpa and Grandma were seated on the porch in their rocking chairs, just rocking away. She looked over at Grandpa and said, "I remember when you used to reach over and take me by the hand." He reached over and rubbed her hand. She said, "I remember when you used to give me a peck on the cheek." He reached over and gave her a kiss on the cheek. She said, "I remember when you used to nibble on my ear." Boy, he jumped up and went in the house. She said, "Where are you going?" He said, "To get my teeth!"

The Star represents Jesus Christ, but the ornaments represent people. I love ornaments. I love looking at them — once Barbara gets them on the tree. I've got an ornament from each year with a picture of my redhead on it. Certainly, when I look at these ornaments, I think about my daughter Savannah. I also think about the lady in our church, Mrs. Ann Freeman, who every year asks me for a picture to make us an ornament. So I think about Mrs. Ann and Mrs. Ann's mother-in-law Ms. Fannie Freeman and how she used to pray for Marvin. Finally, they were so persistent to pray that Marvin came down and got saved! The ornaments represent people.

I have an ornament from the Crystal Cathedral. When I put it on the tree, I don't think about Robert Schuller. I think about the time Stan Daniel and I went to a conference at the Crystal Cathedral. I think about us sleeping in the same room together — me not being able to rest for Stan snoring, but it makes me think about Stan.

Then I got into golfing for awhile, and someone gave me an ornament for that. When I see it, I think about the man who gave it to me and his family. I don't think about the ornaments; I think about the people.

I have one ornament so sacred to me that I won't even let Savannah touch it. I remember being in Pigeon Forge and Barbara and I getting this ornament, then walking to the store next door. It was on a Thursday, and we were getting ready to leave and come home. I saw a sign on the door that said, "Book Signing with Head Coach Phil Fulmer"; but I was leaving. Barbara said, "Listen, Phil would love to meet you. Why don't we stay another day? You can meet the coach and get his autograph. You can get the book and get your picture made with him and talk to him awhile." That was the year the University of Tennessee won the National Championship. When I look at that ornament, I think about Barbara and the trip we made.

I also have a Christmas ornament of the White House. Every year the White House puts out a Christmas ornament. When I look at it, I don't think about George W.; but I think about Mac and Julie Collins, the wonderful people who gave me this ornament. Ornaments represent people, and people are what's really important.

Sometimes we have adverse or difficult times. This is what I've realized that's so amazing. The closer the ornaments are to the Star, the closer they are to each other. Did you ever think about that?

I read about Leonardo da Vinci. He painted the picture of the Lord's Supper; but what you may not know is when he was painting it, he had a conflict with one of his fellow artists. When it got to the face of Judas, he painted that person's face as the face of Judas. True story. Leonardo said he wanted to keep it that way. He wanted that person to have the face of Judas; but every time he would look at the face of Jesus Christ, he couldn't. It was penetrating him like a knife. There was hatred, malice, and bitterness in his heart. He said, "I had to go back and change it." The closer the ornaments are to the star, the closer they will be to each other.

How can a husband love his wife as Christ loves the church as Ephesians 5:25 says and then Ephesians 5:22, "Wives, submit yourselves unto your own husbands, as unto the Lord" and then Ephesians 5:21, "Submitting yourselves one to another in the fear of God"? The only way we can do that is Ephesians 5:18: "And be not drunk with wine, wherein is excess; but be filled with the Spirit." We can't be the husband or the wife or the mother or the father or the grandparent we need to be unless we first have the right relationship with the Star. The closer the ornaments are to the Star, the closer they are to each other. That's why I say to wives, "Don't be jealous of the time your husband spends with God" or to husbands, "Don't be jealous of the time your wife spends with God" because it will make them better wives, husbands, and parents. The star and the ornaments remind us of our relationships.

The tree and the gifts remind us of our redemption. This year you will celebrate Christmas and place your gifts under the tree. God did not place His gift *under* a tree; God placed His gift *on* a tree. Romans 5:8 says, "But God commendeth his love toward us, in that, while we were yet sinners, Christ died for us." John 3:16 says, "For God so loved the world, that he gave his only begotten Son, that whosoever believeth in him should not perish, but have everlasting life." God took heaven's Best — His only begotten Son. God took the Glory of Heaven and said, "Son, You have to go to the low land of sorrow and hang on a tree for the sins of men, women, boys, and girls." We don't deserve Heaven because we're good. We're going to heaven because God is good and Jesus is good and Jesus is kind, and God gave heaven's Best for every one of us!

A mail carrier lost his wife a couple of months before Christmas in a tragic automobile accident and was really hurting. At Christmastime, we need to be keenly aware that there are a lot of people hurting. For many people, the family circle will not be the same as it was last year. This mail carrier went to his supervisor and said, "I want to work all I can. It helps to occupy my time. It helps to occupy my mind."

He was working a few days before Christmas, and there were lots of "Dear Santa…" letters. He made sure they were routed properly. He came to a letter with his return address on it, so he opened it up. It was from his young daughter. It read, "Dear Santa, my mama died and my daddy cries all the time. All he does is cry. Santa, he says only eternity can heal his broken heart. So Santa, would you give my daddy a little bit of eternity this year?" When God gave Jesus, He gave each of us a little bit of eternity.

I watched a documentary on Ronald Reagan. Whether you like him or not, that's not the issue. I just love history. The documentary got to the part where he was shot and his pastor gave this testimony:

"After President Reagan was shot, he was very critical for several days. I went to see him and asked if he was ready to meet God. He said, 'Oh no, I'm not ready to meet God because there is so much I want to see happen. There are so many things I want to do to help people.' 'That's not what I mean. What I mean is are you personally ready to meet God?' He said, 'Yes, I am personally ready to meet God.' I probably dug a little deeper than I should have but asked, 'How do you know you are personally ready to meet God?' I will never forget what he said, 'Because I have a Savior.'"

We place our gifts under the tree; but I thank God, with every fiber of my being, that He placed His gift on the tree for us.

✡